MORE FROM AN ENGLISHMAN IN THE MIDI

MORE FROM AN ENGLISHMAN IN THE MIDI

John P Harris

Illustrations by Franck Poulain

BBC BOOKS

For Sophie, with forty years' love

BY THE SAME AUTHOR:
An Englishman In The Midi (BBC Books, 1991)
Understanding France – a guide for the independent traveller (Macmillan Papermac, 3rd ed. 1991)

Published by BBC Books,
a division of BBC Enterprises Limited,
Woodlands, 80 Wood Lane, London W12 0TT

First Published 1993

ISBN 0 563 36493 9

Set in Meridien Roman by Phoenix Photosetting, Chatham
Printed and bound in England by Clays Ltd, St Ives plc
Cover printed by Clays Ltd, St Ives plc

Contents

TALKING ON RADIO 4

Here are six 'talks' and a selection of articles. The talks were broadcast on BBC Radio 4 towards the end of 1992. The articles appeared in the 1980s in *Le Monde*, *The Times* and *She*, to whose editors my grateful acknowledgements are due. I am also grateful to 'my' BBC producer, Merilyn Harris (no relation, alas).

English friends live in these parts – not in chummy clusters but dotted discreetly around, here and there. They have never objected to my earning occasional cheques by writing about France in general, or about other parts of the hexagon. But revelations about this particular area make them uneasy. They don't want to be colonized. They point out that the Costa Brava is only a couple of hours' drive away in one direction, and Mr Peter Mayle's stamping-ground the same distance in the other direction, and that both areas are much more suitably equipped to deal with rich and poor tourists, fugitives and remittance-men. They claim that there are quite enough Brits here in summer, when friends and relations fill the spare beds (and have been known to sling hammocks), and they suggest that we all have a duty to keep the hinterland between Nîmes and Narbonne on the secret list. I apologize to them. Any inquisitive reader with a map can make an accurate guess at the real-life location of the village and the market town in these pages. I claim unblushingly that any resemblance to existing people and places is wholly coincidental, which means that I have changed names and shuffled things around a bit. I plead in mitigation that I have tried my best to do this area and its inhabitants an injustice by concealing how attractive they really are, and that the discriminating and happy few who buy this book would be welcome anywhere.

Moving to the market town

Last year and the year before that – gosh, how time flies – I was nattering on Radio 4 about life at the centre of a village in Languedoc, which is the inexpensive part of the south of France. Sophie and I bought a small house there in the 1970s, for about half of what we got for selling our previous place. That was an old Cornish farmhouse down a lane where the hedges were bright with raindrops and primroses and Farmer Denham's fifteen unconstipated cows did a return plod to the milking shed twice a day, so you needed gumboots if you went out, except on two or three days a year after a fortnight's drought.

Our children had grown up and gone away to seek their fortune in London. The house was empty without the pitter-patter or thump-thump-thump of feet upon the stairs. There was a problem with dry rot, wet rot and rising damp, the couch grass had got the better of the asparagus bed, and we were tired of being respectable. So we became middle-aged hippies, and hopped it.

The house at the end of the Cornish lane was a mile from anywhere, but in France we were right in the middle of a real working village of eighty inhabitants. We spoke the language fearlessly and our income was at village level or a bit below, so it wasn't difficult to fit in, more or less. Eighty inhabitants is a good size to get to know everyone. We were interested in what went on and how people lived. The years went by in a flash.

But last year we moved. We went all of four miles away, to the nearest town. We still meet a lot of our village friends on Wednesday mornings, because that's market day in the town, so we aren't cut off. The villagers were apprehensive when they learned that our house was going to be up for sale. We were the first foreigners in the village, and it took a while before we seemed to be judged harmless by the majority. You never know. Perhaps we might sell the house on the village square to strangers more outlandish than ourselves: teetotal anti-hunting fanatics or Britons with green hair and safety-pins through their noses (it's wonderful what you learn about other countries on the telly) or indeed to snooty Parisians with cars too big for the streets.

Luckily Madame Escudier, who is one of the village matriarchs, made us a very reasonable offer. Her family has lived in the village since time immemorial in what might be called the big house, and she bought our little one as a wedding present for her daughter Martine. Martine had in fact been happily living an hour's drive away in Montpellier with her friend Pierre for over a year, as people do nowadays even when they come from long-established village families – they can get official certificates of concubinage from the Town Hall, which are handy for Social Security purposes – but marriage is still thought of as a happy ending. So it was nice for everyone, including us.

The town we have moved to has six thousand inhabitants. It's the administrative centre for twenty villages around, with secondary schools and bureaucrats' offices and a hypermarket with a vast car park and even a railway station, which opened in 1863. No trains use the tracks any more except in August, when there's a daily goods train taking table grapes to Paris and elsewhere. Grapes here are what coal is – or was – to South Wales. Most of them are made into wine, oceans of it, but some vineyards specialize in dessert varieties. The first year we were in the village, Sophie and I helped harvest the wine grapes in Henri Poujol's vineyard, but table grapes are not for amateurs from lands where the Brussels sprout flourishes; they have to be snipped with care and laid to rest in nice-looking bunches, in six-kilo trays.

When we lived in the village we were always popping into the town. For three years we spent the winter half of the year in London, working, and we just kept a couple of bicycles at the village. It used to take us thirty-five minutes to cycle to town. That doesn't sound very fast, but round here you're either walking the bike uphill or free-wheeling down – a quarter of an hour of one against one minute of the other, both ways, or so it seems. When we settled permanently we bought a second-hand *deux chevaux*. What luxury to go zoom-zoom to town with two little air-cooled cylinders! They don't make those all-purpose motorized prams any more; motoring has become a very bourgeois activity. I'm glad I had a *deux chevaux* for a while, to rattle and sway to town in.

Why did we move? It was to keep our freedom. We liked the village and the villagers, and we still do. But if you live in a small village you have to have a car. Everybody has one. And 'everybody' means everybody except the old, who may be able to use their legs, but for one reason or another have had to give up driving. Fifteen years ago there were daily buses to the town. Now there's only one a week, on market day. How much longer will the travelling baker, butcher and grocer come and hoot in the square, now that people stock up with basics by driving to the hypermarket? Well, Sophie and I can still drive, and nowadays we have a really bourgeois car with four water-cooled cylinders in which we even potter to London sometimes. But Senior Citizen status is looming. What we can do on foot and by public transport will become important one day.

So now we're in town. Whoever gets up first switches on the kettle, pops round the corner to the baker's and comes back with a still-warm baguette and some croissants before the water's boiled. The buses are five minutes walk away: a dozen a day to Montpellier, from where planes fly direct to London and high-speed trains whizz to Paris. Most things from aspirins to oysters are in the High Street. We don't *have* to have a car. We're free.

The great thing about this town is that there's absolutely nothing special about it. There are no sights, not a single museum or art gallery, and no famous architectural features. No well-known people were ever born here, let alone staying in such a one-horse place after they were old enough to go somewhere more exciting. There are five restaurants, but none of them is in the Michelin guide. In fact there's nothing to attract a tourist, unless for some odd reason he wants to see what ordinary humdrum life is like in an ordinary humdrum small town in the Midi. It isn't smart, but it's convenient, civilized and user-friendly. You can always park the car, and there are no parking meters.

East of the extinct railway station, where the buses go from now, there are two or three hundred modern villas and three blocks of flats. West of the station the early Victorian High Street goes gently uphill until you reach the market place, with a vast thirteenth-century church on one side and the Town Hall on the other. Beyond that there's the old town, rising steeply to a summit where there are the ruins of a fortress. This site isn't important enough to be in the guide-books, there are no attendants and you don't have to pay to go in. If you climb up there by narrow overgrown footpaths you're in an area the size of a football field, among massive ruined walls and broken towers like old teeth. A lot of the stonework disappeared downhill centuries ago, because it's easier to build your house from ready-cut blocks than to go and quarry them yourself and transport them from where the castle-builders hacked them out, a couple of miles away. Recently there's been an attempt to restore some of the towers, but it's still a wild place, with self-sown almond trees, evergreen oaks with leaves like holly, homely blackberry bushes and holes in the ground. If you fall into one of these you find yourself in what was once a store-house or reservoir. Stay above ground, and you get splendid long views of the hills around the town, the distant mountains and the river plain with its covering of vineyards.

The castle is only about eight hundred years old, built ages after the Celts, Greeks and Phoenicians settled here. Later, but long before Julius Caesar made his quick raid into England, the Romans were running the place from their regional capital, Narbonne, fifty miles west. The town is grateful to the emperor Nero, who kindly authorized the market and a forum. When the Roman Empire collapsed, Visigoths took over – when it wasn't Ostrogoths. Then in the eighth century there were Saracens. After they had been driven out, the town became more or less permanently French. There were feudal lords quarrelling, revolts, the ruthless repression of the Albigensian heresy, an expedition by our Black Prince in 1355, and the religious wars, so watch-towers and thick walls with battlements provided a welcome refuge that was regularly used.

If you pick your way down through the honeysuckle and wild sarsaparilla you're in the dark alleys of the old town, and that's where we've moved to, just behind the Town Hall. The alleys are dark because they're narrow, and the buildings, with bits of twelfth-century ramparts in some of their walls, are three or four storeys high. The darkness is a good thing. In summer, from French lunchtime to British teatime, the sun is the enemy. Even mad dogs and Englishmen are unhappy on the motorway, which follows the Roman road from Spain to Italy, and if you park at a shadeless motorway service station to buy a cold drink you turn your car into a solar oven. But the old town stays cool. It can look sinister in parts. A few houses are empty and decrepit. But on the whole it's going up in the world. The council is re-paving some of the little streets with small pink and grey blocks which look nicer than they sound, and the interiors of about half the houses have been ruthlessly modernized by their owners. The interiors only: you're not allowed to mess around with the outside, or to have any sort of roofing except traditional Roman tiles. Car owners can manage. Many of the alleys were built wide enough for a laden donkey to pass another donkey going in the opposite direction, and if pedestrians step aside into doorways a small car can get through. Few alleys are more than fifty yards long, and most of them end in leafy squares where old ladies sit knitting and where there's room for children to play and drivers to park.

Our new house is in what would be a one-way street for donkeys, a yard and a half wide. It's a terrace house, but we can't hear the neighbours because the party walls are six feet thick, good medieval stone. Its street frontage is only twelve feet, but it goes back thirty feet, doubling its width. That's an odd shape, but the houses in the old town do have odd shapes. Some of the ones with wide frontages are shallow, with the house next door making a right-angled turn and continuing round the back of the shallow house. Others have unexpected courtyards in the middle. You can't tell from the street whether a house has two rooms or ten, or whether in the middle there's a secret garden with an orange tree, or half a dozen chickens and a rabbit hutch.

The inside of our house was ripped out by its previous owner, who put in reinforced concrete floors, all covered with tiles. That's usual in these parts. It's cleaner and cooler than carpets, though I'm having some difficulty in preventing Sophie from developing floor-polisher's paranoia. I'm condemned to slippers indoors. I hadn't realized how nice and dirty carpets can get before anyone notices.

The ground floor, again as usual round here, is the cellar floor, with no windows at the wide back end because the ground rises and the cellar burrows into it. There's room for masses of junk, and there's a flashy modern loo and nooks for the deepfreeze and the washing machine. The first floor is a living-room with a high-tech kitchen corner, all electronics and flashing lights. The wide end gives on to a terrace, where we eat whenever the weather's suitable. The terrace looks out on a nice square with plane trees and a fountain-statue in the middle: it's a child or cherub in municipal green, holding a tray over its head. Most of the year the tray holds pots of geraniums. We park our car on that square. We can keep our eye on it, and it's only twenty yards from the front door at the other end of the house, round two corners. The top storey has two bedrooms and a bathroom – and another terrace, made by taking off part of the roof. The two terraces are at opposite ends of the house, so we can choose between east and west according to the time of day and whether we want sun in winter or shade in summer.

And you will appreciate the fact that there are three ways out, if you include getting on to the roof via the top-

storey terrace, and the cellar makes an excellent air raid shelter. Well, perhaps you'll only appreciate those tactical virtues if, like me, you learnt to cope in the Blitz.

I said that most day-to-day things, from aspirins to oysters, are within five minutes' walk, in the High Street. The English are used to aspirins, but many of them boggle at oysters. Such a pity. The French slurp them cheerfully, and in quantity. I can't say that oysters and poverty go together, as they did in Sam Weller's time; but our oyster man comes in his van every Saturday and Sunday, and sets up his stall opposite the Town Hall, and £1.50 will buy you a kilo. That's a dozen medium-sized ones, or nine whoppers, or 20 little 'uns. Saturdays and Sundays are relatively leisured days when anyone in this ordinary small town might think of starting his dinner with a plate of oysters, a squeeze of lemon and a glass of cool white wine. The local white wine is fifty pence a litre if you take it away straight from the pump, and the oyster man will probably give you the lemon free. Some rye bread and butter, and you couldn't be better off at the Ritz, because you're at home, and after another course or two you can have a siesta absolutely gratis, whereas at the Ritz you have to pay for a bed. Ah, you say, but at the Ritz they open the oysters for you. So does the kind oyster man, if there isn't a queue. He lends you a polystyrene platter, puts a little seaweed on it to look pretty, flips open your oysters, lays them out in concentric circles and covers the lot with cling-film. Carry them home carefully, and there you are. Of course anyone ought to be able to open an oyster, and prehistoric man did it without an oyster-knife. Allow an hour for your first dozen, and blood, sweat and tears. By your twelfth dozen, if you're like me, you'll be down to ten minutes, unwounded. But the oyster man is quicker. Ah, the pleasures of town life!

Where we are now

As I said, the great thing about our little town is that it's absolutely humdrum and ordinary: no sights, no posh hotels or chic restaurants. But we do see tourists in the summer nowadays. They come to the outskirts to load up at the hypermarket, and sometimes they venture inwards to mingle with the natives at banks, chemists' and the queue in the post office. But they aren't based in the town. They live a quarter of an hour's drive away, at a big modern camp site with hot showers and power points for caravans. It's become popular in the last ten years, especially with the Dutch and the Germans. It's at Lake Salagou.

Lake Salagou comes lower in the holiday lake league than Windermere or Lake Maggiore, but much higher than Lake Wobegon. Lake Wobegon is only 678 acres, according to the book. Ours is four times that size. It straggles irregularly among low mountains, with vineyards – of course – on the lower slopes, and trees for shade. Most of the soil around is a deep red, and it looks wild and beautiful. It's a good place for sailing and wind-surfing and swimming, and not bad for fishing, and has been much improved by a recent ban on all forms of motor boat – an issue that caused heated debate in the town council. The speed-and-noise lobby was led by Monsieur Espinasse, who sells motor-bikes and mopeds and outboard motors. It was defeated by the fishing, swimming and wind-surfing lobby, and by the picknicking-with-siesta lobby, to the disgust of our young neighbour Pierre Combadazou. He had discovered the joys of jet-skiing down at the coast and was all set to start a Salagou jet-ski club. Now he contents himself with cross-country motor-bike scrambling, up in the garrigue behind the village, and at Lake Salagou you can hear the nightingales and the cicadas as you float in the unpolluted water.

Lake Wobegon, supposed to be in Minnesota, is more famous than Lake Salagou, but that's because it's all in the fertile imagination of Mr Garrison Keillor. Lake Salagou is really there, and you can find it on the map. But I'm not giving you the name of the town. That allows me to change people's names, thus confusing the issue in the unlikely event of anyone from down there listening. On the other hand there must be an awful lot of lakes in Minnesota like Lake Wobegon, deep and wet long before the first Red Indian or Eskimo put a toe in their waters, whereas Lake Salagou wasn't there twenty years ago. You need a modern map to find it. It was made by damming the River Salagou. There's a fine dam, over half a mile long, containing one and a half million tons of rock. The whole job: buying up the land to be flooded, making the dam and making new roads – you can see the old main road sloping down into the water – all that cost seven million pounds. The French Ministry of Agriculture paid over half.

The idea was to get an irrigation scheme going. Farmers would stop being dependent on vines and grapes and wine, of which there's a vast surplus every year. It gets withdrawn from the market at rock-bottom prices, too low to keep the wine people happy but too high for the people who have to manage the Common Agricultural Policy. So the locals would uproot their vines and plant – what? I don't know. Apples and pears perhaps, or peach trees, or kiwis, or carrots. For one mysterious reason and another it didn't happen. The irrigation canals were never built and the vineyards are still there.

So is Lake Salagou a failure, like the Great African Groundnut Scheme that shuddered to a halt in 1950 after costing the British taxpayer many times the price of a respectable dam? I don't think it is. The locals, despite the ritual groans and moans that accompany growing anything anywhere for a living, still seem to think that growing grapes is what God put man on earth to do. After all, what did that able and virtuous ecologist Noah do when the waters had subsided and he'd sent all those smelly animals out of the way? He planted a vineyard. And the lake has provided this super camp site at one corner, and a sailing school, and lots of fun for windsurfers from all over Europe as well as from our town. And then there are the Canadairs.

Sometimes a siren sounds, and everybody who is in the lake has to get out of it sharpish. A Canadair aircraft flies low over the lake and scoops up a ton or so of water and then goes and dumps it on a forest fire. Such fires are alas fairly frequent in the Midi in the summer. Sometimes they are started by nutcases, called pyromaniacs, or by small children who want to see a Canadair, but usually it's pure carelessness, like people from the North throwing a lighted cigarette-end out of the car or defying the great big notices and lighting a fire to grill sausages for a picnic. No naked flames in forests, please! It's reported that once an obstinate young lady carried on swimming, was scooped up by a Canadair and dumped on a forest fire sixty miles away. That's a good story, but it never happened. It's one of those legends, like the old one about the English couple who went for a motoring holiday in the Midi and brought Granny with them. One hot afternoon Granny dies in the car. They cover her with a rug and drive to the nearest police station, to report their sad loss. When they come out, they've lost the car as well. The thief didn't stop to look under the rug. No body, no death certificate, no inheritance of Granny's fortune. Don't believe it. But never cover Granny with a rug.

Now let's get back to the town itself. The market-place is a wide square shaded by plane trees taller than the buildings. On the left is the Mairie: the Town Hall. It's a building of no architectural distinction, basically dating from the middle of the last century, but with its façade tarted up to look vaguely modern: the Victorian curlicues and caryatids and shallow decorative wrought-

iron balconies that you can see on the other four-storey buildings in the square have been wiped off and replaced by a plain ochre-coloured façade with plate-glass doors. It looks quite cheerful in the sun, though, because at third-floor level it flies its three flags: the French blue-white-and-red, the flag of Europe with its circle of gold stars on a blue background and the regional flag. This carries the Occitan cross, a decorated cousin of the Maltese cross, yellow on a red ground. You can see crude versions of this cross as graffiti here and there, with OC written below. These were paint-sprayed, mostly in the 1970s, by young people who thought it would be a good idea to start up a Free Occitania movement.

Occitania, *Occitanie*, is roughly that part of the Midi that lies between Provence and the Spanish border, and Occitan is the local language. It's really the same as Provençal. It almost died out in the last century, though Provençal writers like Mistral tried to keep it going. A few old people still speak it, and enthusiasts run classes in it. It can even be studied at school, as an optional exam subject, but very few pupils take that option. They're a practical lot down here: English, Spanish and German lead to a more prosperous career, and French with a Midi accent is everybody's mother tongue and has been for a century. But the Occitan flag is the flag of the region, and regarded with a special affection when Brussels – that's the EEC flag – or Paris – the French tricolore – seem to be making regulations that interfere with the Midi way of life.

Just in front of the Mairie there's a stone column, and on the top is a metal bust of Jean-Antoine Peyrottes, a respectable-looking gentleman with mutton-chop whiskers, painted in dark green. You could call it town council green: you see it everywhere in the town on all municipal metallic surfaces, and I'm told there's enough of it in stock to keep us going until well into the next millennium. Peyrottes was a local man who wrote poems in Occitan, in praise of the town. He died in 1858, and the inscription on the column shows that this little monument was erected some years after his death by a kindly municipal council. His heart was in the right place, but he wasn't a brilliant poet. Nobody in the rest of France today has read him or even heard of him, and in fact the only people in the town who know his name are those who have gone to the trouble of reading the worn lettering on the little column. For the rest, he's just a dark green head with mutton-chop whiskers, an anonymous local worthy who probably did something some time.

Well, he loved the place and did his best. I lift my hat to him as I pass.

Talking of monuments, there's a British war grave three miles from Lake Salagou – three miles as the crow flies, that is, if he or she flies over a mountain ridge a thousand feet above lake level. It's in the cemetery of a tiny village in a strange place called a *cirque dolomitique*, and if I look that expression up in the dictionary I get 'dolomitic cirque,' which doesn't help much. Geological events have created a landscape of great jagged knobbly rock towers, as if a mad giant had played at building a city and then given up in a temper, leaving it to erosion to put the finishing touches to a sort of Wild West fantasy, ideal for prehistoric monsters – and in fact a brontopus has left his fossilized footprints not far away.

It was also ideal as a defensive HQ for a resistance group in the last war. In August 1944, just after the Allied landings in Provence, eight British SOE people, with dozens of containers of arms and ammunition, landed near here by parachute to join forces with the maquis band. The orders for the Germans, notably a Panzer division based between here and the Spanish border, were to belt as fast as possible to the battlefields of northern France before they were cut off. Paris was being liberated at the time, but France was still to see months of fighting. Allied High Command wanted the Germans' dash northwards to be slowed down as much as possible, by denying them the use of easy roads along the coastal plain and up the Rhône valley. Allied planes bombed the main roads, and the SOE and the maquis blew up bridges and laid ambushes. So the Panzer division and the others had to go via twisting mountain roads, where they were attacked and delayed by other maquis groups through hundreds of miles of hard going.

Such tactics called for a certain amount of heroism among the locals en route. I mean, if I heard that an SS division was coming through the place I lived in, and that their sole ambition was to get north as quickly as possible and never come back, I would be tempted to say 'Hear hear! And the quicker the better' – instead of trying to thwart them by blowing up the bridge and sniping at them with a Sten gun. Especially as the Germans shot, or hanged, not only captured maquis irregulars but also local hostages.

Our eight SOE men and the maquis did their job, and they were the first Allied troops to enter Montpellier. Except, that is, for Peter Fowler and two gendarmes, who had been coming back to the *cirque dolomitique* on a motor-cycle and sidecar from observing German tanks on one of the roads along the plain.

A company of trainee SS troops were making their retreat along a minor road on bicycles – yes, push-bikes;

they were short of transport – and they heard the noise of the motor-bike, which could only mean other Germans or the resistance. So they lay in wait, opened fire and killed the three of them in a vineyard by the road. There's an obelisk there now, with inscriptions in French and in English. Germain Maurin is one of our friends in the village where we lived until we moved to town. He was sixteen at the time. That night he drove the three bodies in his father's lorry from the vineyard on the plain to the maquis HQ in the cirque, and next day they were buried in the little churchyard. Soon after the war the remains of the two gendarmes were moved to their home town, but Peter Fowler, aged twenty-five, is still there among the towering rocks and the arbutus trees, and his grave is carefully looked after by the villagers.

So there you are. I said that our humdrum one-horse town is completely devoid of tourist attractions, and now I've mentioned a couple of places within a quarter of an hour's drive that attract tourists of all nationalities, and quite right too. And the citizens of our town don't mind tourists at all. In fact, as long as they don't try to squeeze in front of them in the queue at the post office, they quite like them. Don't be afraid! Monsieur J.A. Peyrottes was right, a hundred and fifty years ago. We love this town too. Three cheers for Occitania!

Keeping fit

When one starts thinking about health and fitness one realizes that one is not quite on the level of Jane Fonda or Arnold Schwarzenegger, physically, and indeed that one has – if one thinks long enough – symptoms. So let's start right away with my friend Madame Faugerat the chemist.

She has a typical French chemist's shop at the top of the High Street, with a green neon cross flashing on and off like a lighthouse above the automatic plate glass doors. It's different from a British chemist's. For one thing, it says 'Pharmacie Faugerat' outside, not the name of a chain. Chain chemists would be illegal in France. The place has to be owned and run personally by a qualified pharmacist – it's a six-year course taken after the equivalent of A Levels – and he, or more usually she, is personally responsible for identifying the forty or fifty kinds of succulent toadstool that people bring in, and warning them off the dangerous ones; and for administering simple first aid and for sternly directing you to the doctor if there's any doubt – and for checking that he hasn't absent-mindedly prescribed two things which, mingling in your inside, could produce a melodramatic surprise.

Neither at Madame Faugerat's nor at any other French chemist's can you buy photographic equipment, cassettes, compact discs, saucepans, picture postcards, toys, Christmas decorations or wrapped sandwiches to take away. On the other hand, you can't buy aspirins or cough mixture at the grocer's or the supermarket. Madame Faugerat makes a reasonable profit out of pharmaceuticals – you need a carrier bag to take away the average French doctor's prescription – and a greater profit from what they call parapharmacy: vitamins, beauty creams, dodges for stopping smoking and suchlike. Although the French love getting powerful and expensive medicines prescribed for them, they also have a soft spot for harmless homeopathic remedies and for drinking infusions of leaves or roots that were esteemed by their great-grandmothers. The last time I was there I counted two hundred different herbs in nice little packs with pictures on them, neatly arranged in alphabetical order. They do no harm, says Madame Faugerat, and sometimes they do you good. Even in these days of the pill, she says that *armoise*, which the dictionary tells me is artemisia or mugwort, has a hopeful following.

Down at the bottom of the High Street is Doctor Dupont's *Laboratoire Médical*. That's where you go when your doctor thinks it would be a good idea for you to have a blood test or something like that. They're keen on blood tests. For one thing, it helps the circulation of money in the right circles. In France you pay cash for such things, as with the doctor and the chemist, and then you get about three-quarters back from the Social Security office, or more if you've got something long-lasting and nasty. Perhaps because of this method of payment, the results of blood tests, as well as X-ray photographs and so forth, are the property of the patient, and you get your own copy before you go along to see what your doctor thinks. So you can see for yourself what you've got in the shape of cholesterol and corpuscles and whatnot floating around inside. And as it says what are the normal limits for all the oddments they test you for, you can spend a fascinating hour checking your score and comparing it with what your friends and neighbours got last time, before going over it with the doctor. 'Don't worry!' said Dr Tessier to me last month, 'Cholesterol is good for you!' I do like that man. The *Laboratoire Médical* is quite elegant, and the personnel kindly make you feel a brave warrior when you've given them a teaspoonful of the precious fluid.

Up near the church there's a health food store. I've never gone inside, and I haven't seen anybody else doing so. When the locals think about health they think of the doctor and a bagful of pills, ointments and aerosol inhalers from Madame Faugerat, or they think of jogging (called *le jogging*) and jumping up and down. There's an aerobics place in a side-street advertising such goodies as *le stretching* and *le body-building*. Yes, they use English words, or probably American – the Jane Fonda influence. Here, word for word, is an ad. from the local paper:

L'Association Athletic Must Center de Montpellier propose un week-end Master Class de Fitness . . . Still, this health food shop and its sad-looking owner have been there for the last five years, so someone must buy the tins of tofu, the cartons of sugar-free biscuits made of bran, the wholemeal spaghetti, the pots of dried powdered seaweed and of royal jelly from the best bees, all waiting dustily in the window. I'm fascinated by a box of capsules of concentrated mare's milk, just small enough to be swallowed by a determined health-foodist. According to what it says on the box, it's foolish to try coping with this hard world without gulping a capsule of concentrated mare's milk twice a day. But at sixty capsules for seventeen pounds I think I'll stick to steak and chips.

Of course, they say that things start in America, take ten years to get to England and then reach France ten years after that. Unfair to France, I must say, at any rate when it comes to smart punctual high-speed trains. But perhaps it's true in the matter of food, and one day the health food man will look healthy and wealthy as well as wise.

Just now, though, London comes as a bit of a shock. I was there recently trying to find bread and butter at a big supermarket. It was hard work, pounding along yards and yards of shelving filled with brown bread, black bread, grey bread and guaranteed breadless bread before I could find the white stuff. Butter, made of nothing but cream entirely produced by genuine cows, lurked shamefacedly among all the varieties of what up-to-date Londoners spread on their chunks of fibrous roughage. I saw stuff called vegetarian cheese. Now what can that be? I'm out of touch.

In London our daughter proudly served us wholemeal macaroni. The last time I'd had that was in Italy, in 1945, at the home of a Neapolitan violinist who apologized deeply, explaining that violinists in the ranks of the orchestra didn't earn enough to get the real stuff on the black market. And he had thought that there was something to be said for Mussolini until he launched Italy into war, death, destruction and wholemeal pasta.

Don't worry, if you're keen. Consciously virtuous foodstuffs can be found at the local hypermarket, but it's the reverse of the London situation. You'll find them hidden among the expensive exotic delicacies like chocolate-coated ants, pumpernickel, pilpil and Worcester Sauce. The locals still stick to their traditional diet, eaten because they like it, and they live a few months longer than the average Briton.

Many of them do in fact like non-white sorts of bread to go with special dishes – rye bread with oysters, for example. My favourite baker, Monsieur Bonacini, bakes a good selection. His grandfather, also a baker, was one

of those Italians who got on the wrong side of Mussolini and settled in France – like the parents of that fine and very French actor, the late Yves Montand. Bonacini, I'm glad to say, was born long after Yves Montand, and looks as though he can carry on prosperously for the next twenty years turning out not only the usual long crusty white baguettes, but also wholemeal bread with or without added bran for what the French call *le transit intestinal,* brown bread with chopped walnuts in it, croissants and ordinary bread in odd shapes when he's in the mood. He's a dab hand at turning out alligators.

However, Sophie and I once got to know brown rice intimately. It was fifteen years ago, after we'd settled into the village we lived in before we moved to this town. We made friends with Jack and Maxine, an Anglo-American couple living some ten miles away on an even thinner and shorter shoe-string than we had. She's an artist, and he had dropped out of a school of architecture. They had come to the Midi with just enough money to buy a ruin and an acre of vegetable garden. And how they worked! They helped out as casual labour, reconstructed their ruin and lived mainly on their vegetables – and brown rice. They are doing well nowadays. Maxine's pictures are in demand. They sold their nicely rebuilt ruin to a rich Belgian and reconstructed a better one, and in the kitchen they've gone French. But in those days they needed a fifty-kilo sack – that's a hundredweight – of brown rice every two months. Rice is very successfully grown sixty miles away from here, in the Camargue (where they have wild horses as well). Maxine and Jack had a beat-up old van. If you're going to drive to the

Camargue to fetch untreated rice from the producer, you might as well fetch a lot. So they were keen on getting orders from their friends. They put us down for a sack. It was much cheaper than getting it in little packets from health food shops, not that we did, and equally brimful of minerals, vitamins, fibres, good vibrations of yin (or was it yang? – terribly zen, anyway) and guaranteed to give gymnastic activity to the alimentary canal from one end to the other.

We found that half a pound twice a week, yang or yin, was as much as we could get through. So there was two years' supply in our sack.

After six weeks Sophie found some tiny long-nosed beasties in the ration. We showed them to Madame Martin, the schoolmistress. Ah yes, she said: she remembered them well from the war, when they got into her parents' hidden stock of dried beans. They were *charançons,* and there was something you could get from the chemist for them.

So we went to see Madame Faugerat. She told us to put the rice in a big plastic dustbin, put some cotton wool soaked in *sulfure de carbone* in a saucer on top – nasty-smelling stuff, she sold us a bottle – and put the lid on tight. So we did, and it worked. If you have the same trouble, *charançons* are weevils and *sulfure de carbone* is carbon disulphide. Twice a week we spread our ration on a tray and picked out the little corpses. Then we had to go away for a couple of months. When we came back there was a happy family of well-fed rats in the cellar. They had gnawed through the black plastic lid of the dustbin. So we learned how to deal with rats as well as weevils.

Sophie and I sorted through one half-pound of brown rice, discarding bits of chewed plastic and rat droppings as well as dead weevils, and decided that the simple life was not for us. We had three-quarters of the sack left. We gave it to Monsieur Estelle, who keeps poultry, and he gave us a couple of nice fat free-range guinea fowl.

My present keep-fit sport is going fishing, with a collapsible stool. Next door to Madame Faugerat's is the fishing tackle and shot-gun shop. That's where I buy my maggots, five francsworth at a time, a big cupful that Monsieur Nadal scoops up from the bran tub. Maggots soon turn into a less useful stage in their life cycle in hot weather, so I keep a plastic box of them in the fridge. That's one of the reasons why I love my wife Sophie. There aren't many female companions who will let you do that. Years ago, when I was young, I was told that gentlemen used flies, not maggots, but I've gone native. The perch in our lake and the chub in our river are so used to avoiding being caught with maggots that surprising them with a queer foreign dry fly would be unsporting.

There's more profit in shot-guns and ammunition, and dinky little kits of prod-rods and scoops for making your own cartridges. In the village where we used to live, shooting was definitely not a gentlemanly sport. In fact that was the whole point of the French Revolution, according to my friend Monsieur Gal, who liked to keep the supply of thrushes in his wife's deepfreeze regularly topped up. Before the Revolution only the aristocrats went shooting – and they kept masses of greedy pigeons in dovecots in the grounds of their châteaux, which fed themselves fat on the peasants' crops. And the peasants weren't allowed to use even a catapult on them. So since 1789 the downtrodden country folk have been blazing away, and any surviving aristo stays indoors and keeps his head down. Well, that's the sentiment. The village belongs to a group that buys pheasants and lets them loose at the beginning of the shooting season, and as the pheasants have been brought up on a pheasant-breeding farm they trot forward wagging their tails whenever they see a chap emerging from behind a bush.

Wild boar are a different proposition. They do their own breeding and can be a nuisance in cold winters, coming down from the hills and digging up vine-stumps. You need a lot of men for a wild boar shoot, and they use whacking big bullets. Only one person gets killed at this game for every two or three thousand that get killed by motor-cars, but all the same, Sophie doesn't go out walking on the hills during the shooting season, and when I do I wear a bright red pullover and whistle loudly in the hope that I don't look like a wild boar even in the eyes of the most enthusiastic shot. Luckily when spring comes the shooting season is over, and one can hunt wild asparagus in safety.

Down the High Street

Outside the Town Hall on the left, as I said, there's the bust of our local poet, Jean-Antoine Peyrottes. On the right is a more impressive piece of statuary: a mythological lady in municipal green striking an enthusiastic pose and waving a jug. She's on top of a carved stone fountain. Eight spouts in the shape of lions' heads gush into a wide stone trough that goes all round the base. Before there was mains water, people came here with buckets and water-pots. They still come, but with bottles these days, filling them with drinking water straight from the spouts. The mains water is quite all right, but people with sensitive taste-buds can detect a faint tang of chlorine, so they prefer to fill up here with pure spring water. It's tested, of course. You're safe enough in France when you see one of these decorative fountains, unless it has a prominent notice on it saying EAU NON POTABLE – not drinking water. One of the nice things about France is that, despite fast food and convenience dishes from the deepfreeze, a lot of ordinary people take ordinary food and drink seriously. I don't mean foie gras and vintage wine in cobwebbed bottles, but bread and eggs and drinking water. Many of the townsfolk look down their noses at neighbours who buy well-advertised bottled mineral waters. In 1990, which is the latest year I've got statistics for, the French drank ninety-seven litres of those, per head, while the British drank seven. My neighbours claim that water from this handsome fountain is much better, as well as being free.

They do drink water in the Midi. If you go by best-sellers written by northern foreigners about life in southern France, you'd think that the average local lives in a permanent alcoholic haze. The only drunks I've seen in this town are northerners on holiday. It's true that there's a bit of a drugs problem in Montpellier, our nearest big town, where the police make regular swoops on dealers, but that affects only a fringe minority. There was one drunkard in the village where we lived for fifteen years, an old man who was said to get through six litres of plonk a day. He died soon after we came – of lung cancer actually, and he was a non-smoker, which was unfortunate for people who like to take a high moral line, but that didn't prevent the villagers pointing the finger of scorn and being quite genuinely shocked while he was alive.

They're a sober lot down here, and the statistics prove it. The top regions in France for alcoholism are Brittany and the north from Calais to Alsace-Lorraine. The lowest are Languedoc and the Midi-Pyrénées region, which also

have a well-below-average suicide rate. Provence is below average for alcoholism, but above Languedoc. Here, anyone seriously interested in getting sozzled can fill up his jerrycan with decent red wine for the price of a couple of hamburgers, but the average local seems content with a glass or two with his dinner; and if he goes to the café to sit in the shade of the plane trees for a chat with his friends, he makes one apéritif last an hour or more.

Opposite the Town Hall is the church. It's a vast structure, like a castle in parts, with battlements and a hundred-foot-high watch tower. Back in the fourteenth century it formed part of the town's defences. Between the church and the Town Hall there's a large area: a street with wide pavements under the trees. And there are benches, which seem usually bagged by male old age pensioners. They get a grandstand view of everyone arriving for weddings and funerals, and if nothing like that is going on there's always the pleasure of analysing the passers-by.

On Wednesday mornings the analysts have to go somewhere else because of the market. It occupies all this area and the first hundred yards of the streets leading to it. They are closed to traffic for the occasion. There are all the usual market things: oysters and octopus as well as soles and crabs; chickens and rabbits in the full range from alive to oven-ready; fruit and veg, hams from the mountains, ironmongery, cheap clothes and shoes . . . When the hypermarket opened on the outskirts eight years ago, with its car park and computerized cash desks, I thought the real market would dwindle away. But not a bit of it. Peoplc who've got time like to spend it comparing produce and prices, and bumping into friends who've come in from outlying villages. Tourists come from the camp site in the summer, and then sellers of souvenirs made in the Far East turn up on the watch for them. Summer or winter there's a crowd, except on the one or two Wednesdays a year when it rains. We get the same annual rainfall as London, but instead of rationing itself out, little and often, it comes in giant bucketfuls on a few days in spring and autumn.

Except on Wednesday mornings, whenever the weather's decent, chairs and tables and multicoloured parasols come out on the market square – one lot from a café which is also the favoured place for card-players, indoors, and the other lot from the Pizzeria Pinocchio. It makes rather dim pizzas, at least compared with what you get in any Italian small town or the ones you can make yourself with a lump of bread dough. But it does good business the year round with youngish people who don't want to devote the greater part of their two-hour lunch break to a time-consuming meal in one of the town's five traditional restaurants. Unlike big towns, we haven't got a hamburger joint yet.

The High Street runs down from the market place, a quarter of a mile to the station. It's wide, quite unlike the Old Town. The buildings are standard French of 150 years ago: four-storey blocks, with wrought-iron balconies, shutters on each side of the tall windows, mansard roofs, and caryatids or other bits of sculpture here and there. The bottom floor is shops, the other floors are quite large flats. That's where the bourgeoisie lived – and some still do – before post-war people started wanting an English-type villa, with front and back garden and perhaps a swimming pool. Those are on the outskirts, and you need a car to come to town. Parking is usually easy, and there are no parking meters or anything like that, though there is the French system of parking on one side of the street in the first half of the month, and the other side in the second half – with a certain amount of fuss and bother at 9 p.m. on the 15th and on the last day of the month, when in theory you shift the car briskly. But down here the police aren't fussy about that, and in practice you've got until seven or eight in the morning when the shops and offices open.

The first shop we come to belongs to a *visagiste*, or face specialist. She will pluck out your eyebrows and stick on your eyelashes and keep you topped up with Chanel No. 5. According to a notice in the window she will also provide you with 'supernatural' nails, *ongles surnaturelles*. They're supernatural in the sense that they're glued on over your natural ones. The *visagiste* has been there for the last ten years. When we first knew the town the shop was a grocer's. In fact there were seven other small grocers in the High Street, and they have all turned into small clothes shops. I used to wonder how they can keep going, because one sees hardly anyone buying anything there except at sale time. But it doesn't cost much to keep a shop here. The clothes shops seem to be run by widows who like to have a place where friends can drop in, and perhaps a garment a day is enough. Or they are wives whose husbands do a heftier job. Monsieur Vernet is a blacksmith who made some railings for us. He sweats away in his smithy behind his wife's High Street clothes shop.

I'd like to think that I've been talking about significant differences between life in England and in the Midi, but perhaps it's basically the difference between small-town life anywhere and big city life anywhere: Chipping Sodbury and London, Wobegon (Minnesota) and New York. Anyway, here's the bank, and there *is* a difference.

When I go to a bank in England I can wander in free as air during the short time the place is open, but if I want to do business I'm separated from the cashier by a bullet-proof glass window. Conversation isn't easy through a little hole in the glass. So we don't catch each other's colds, and our fingers don't meet either; we shunt bits of paper and cash through a slot. Safe and hygienic, but not sociable.

My bank down here opens at a quarter past eight and stays open until five, except of course between twelve and two. Time is money, but people have to eat – and sandwiches won't do. I go through one bullet-proof glass door, and four feet further on I'm stopped by another one. I have to press a button. If one of the cashiers likes the look of me, he presses his button and the second door opens. I gather that if they find me absolutely revolting, coming in or going out, they can press a different button and there I am, trapped between the two doors until the police arrive.

But once I'm inside it's nice. I lean over the counter to shake hands with Monsieur Bastide. I've known him ever since we bought our previous house, in the village four miles away, and we have friends in common and views and comments to exchange. Well, not if there are a lot of people waiting. Then we just shake hands, enquire rapidly about each other's health, and get on with it. Don't go shaking hands the first time you meet a cashier. But you should by the third or fourth time, unless you want to be thought snooty or a cold fish. That goes for the tax man too.

French bureaucracy has a fearsome reputation, but

when you actually meet a bureaucrat, difficulties can melt away. I remember the first time I wrestled with a set of French income tax forms. In France you pay tax this year on last year's income, and they have the exotic habit of starting the financial year on the 1st January instead of the 6th April, so if you have to deal with the two countries' tax men because you have bits of income arising in both, you can easily find your wits getting addled even if, like me, you haven't got much income worth taxing. So I went to an accountant in this town. No good, because he'd never seen the dreaded pink form, no 2047, which deals with foreign income, and didn't understand it. So as a last resort I went to the tax inspector, in a bigger town twenty minutes' drive away. A charming fellow. He helped me fill up my forms in no time, and told me what to do so as to have to pay almost no tax the next year. Never write in France: go to see them. I have the impression that British tax inspectors like to be at least two hundred miles away from their clients, if that's the right word, and are not terribly pleased when one of them drops in.

Now we come to the matter of keeping in touch, exemplified by the paper shop, opposite, and the post office further down. A lot goes on in the paper shop because it's the official place for cigarettes and tobacco, car licences and various sorts of betting tickets. There are no bookmakers, or indeed football pools as such, in France. That sort of thing is a state monopoly. In the paper shop you see people buying cards on which they hope to get rich by predicting the numbers that will pop up in the shape of what look like ping-pong balls on the telly tonight, and if they know which will be the first five horses in a race, in the right order, they collect an embarrassing amount of money. If they know only the first three, in the wrong order, it might pay for a good lunch. This is where I buy my copy of *Le Monde* every morning. It's an afternoon paper. But you can get it in the afternoon or indeed on the day of publication only if you're in Paris or a few favoured big towns. So, like other benighted provincials, I buy yesterday afternoon's *Monde* in the morning. There is one enormous snag about this. *Le Monde* has lumbered itself with the custom of giving itself the following day's date. So Parisians read tomorrow's *Monde* with their after-lunch coffee, while we get what claims to be today's paper but isn't. The paper itself says things like 'See Tuesday's issue, dated Wednesday' and when it says 'yesterday' or 'today' or 'tomorrow' you have to do a bit of thinking, because it can mean one thing or the other.

In terms of newspaper quantity for cash, one is better off north of the Channel. Taking ten francs to the pound, my Parisian paper costs me 70p, and it's much smaller than any of the British quality papers, partly because advertisers prefer the telly. There's a regional paper costing 40p, good for crime, sport, the horoscope and comic strips, but nothing like *Le Monde* for international news. But it's essential for the deaths page. It isn't done to die without anything from four to ten column-inches in the local paper, to let all your friends know. There's a standard style that starts off with the name of your town or village, and the names of all the towns and villages you've ever lived in, or where your relations live. The least you can do when someone you've vaguely known dies in your town is to sign the book. It's an exercise book on a table draped in black, outside the dead person's door. So you have to keep an eye on the local paper.

When I lived up a muddy lane miles from anywhere in Cornwall my London paper came with the milk at seven in the morning. The only way to get your paper delivered in France is by postal subscription. Oddly enough that's cheaper than buying it at the paper shop, because the French Post Office has to carry papers at a loss-making rate. In my case that would mean getting my Paris lunch-time paper at about eleven the next day, and the issue of Saturday, dated Sunday, would come half way through Monday. Bah! There's a near-monopoly that has a stranglehold on transporting papers. That seems to be another reason behind the price at the paper shop. As I said, you don't know how lucky you are in the UK. You can get my favourite French paper, 70p in France, for 85p in England, just a third dearer – and no later than I get it. But a 40p British paper, a day late down here, costs me £1.20, and a fat Sunday £2.40, usually without the colour supplement.

So French dailies are smaller and dearer, and have smaller circulations. A compensation is that France has a fine range of weeklies, both middlebrow and highbrow. That's where many people get their political commentary and their features from, and they rely on the telly for up-to-date news. And if you can watch the telly from eight to nine in the morning – except when children are on holiday and get cartoons – you can see TV news from

England, Germany, Russia, Spain and Italy, video-recorded an hour or two earlier, with French subtitles, and with comments by a bright multi-lingual Englishman, Alex Taylor.

Now for the post office. After you've crossed the *Boulevard Gambetta* the High Street turns into a wide avenue of plane trees, for pedestrians only. It leads to the bus station, but buses and cars have to filter round another way, which is the right priority for comfortable living. There's the post office, and a café with tables and chairs in the open for seven or eight months of the year, and rocking-horses and toddlers' slides that the council put up last year; and of course benches. Our town is rich in benches: winter benches in sunny corners out of the wind, and summer benches in the shade. It's a poor life if you have no time to sit and stare and exchange comments.

But in the post office one is less philosophical about the passing minutes. There are three counters, which isn't too many for six thousand inhabitants. They are manned, or rather personed, by methodical official ladies who have to do all the things their British opposite numbers have to do, and a lot more involving computer terminals and complicated forms. I suppose ten minutes' waiting one's turn isn't a grave hardship, and one ought to emit vibrations of love instead of loathing towards the person in front who needs everything explained three times, very slowly. But still. . . .

Never, by the way, never go to a big French post office if all you need is stamps, unless you like using sledgehammers to crack nuts. They're on sale at every tobacconist's, and the turnover is quicker there.

But small post offices are all right. The village, four miles from here, where we used to live was too small for a post office, so I usually went to one in the next village. Sometimes I walked, half an hour each way, along a hillside lane, traffic-free except for an occasional tractor on vineyard business. On a clear winter's day you could see Mount Canigou, on the Spanish border a hundred miles away, covered with snow; and there were wild flowers along the way, to be looked up in the book when I got home; and in their seasons fallen almonds and walnuts to be scavenged. And sometimes I drive there now. Time-and-motion study suggests that I would do better to queue at the town post office, but cost-benefit analysis gives good marks to the village post office because it's a pleasure to call there. Monsieur Cros runs it, with a staff of one part-timer, his wife, who delivers letters on foot. One counter for four hundred inhabitants is a much better ratio than three for six thousand, and Monsieur Cros is a nice man. He takes a kindly interest in my affairs, lets me choose big beautiful stamps when I write to America, provides string for me when he doesn't think my parcels are ship-shape, and gives me useful non-postal advice like where to go if I want a car battery at a discount. Just occasionally there's another customer, and then Monsieur Cros introduces us. I'm his tame Englishman, and as most other customers will have had something like a second cousin who went to England twenty years ago as a child, there's the start of a basis for conversation – usually about the weather. Don't try telling elderly

French people that their picturesque notions about the Dickensian London fog are out of date. If I've explained the Clean Air Act of 1955 to them once, I've explained it fifty times. They don't believe it; they LIKE to think of you poking your smoky coal fires and then groping your way out into the pea soup. Well, there are some equally strange picturesque ideas going around in England about France, but we won't go into that.

Just at the moment Monsieur Cros is disappointed in me. I've been sending instalments of a manuscript to a London publisher. Each bit weighs in at around 125 grammes: five or six ounces. Now it costs 18F to send a letter weighing between 100 and 250 grammes to England, but between 50 and 100 grammes it's only 6F 20. So he pointed out that if I were to split my letter into two, there would be two 6F 20 letters: a saving of 5F 60 on the total, or say 5F 50 if we allow ten centimes for the extra envelope. Just why officialdom wants to encourage people to send two little letters instead of one medium-sized one is a mystery to me and to Monsieur Cros. Perhaps it's to keep postmen busy. Anyway, I've carried on posting the stuff in five-ounce chunks as I write it, wasting over 5F each time through sheer laziness, and blushing at Monsieur Cros's reproachful silence as I put the envelope on the scales.

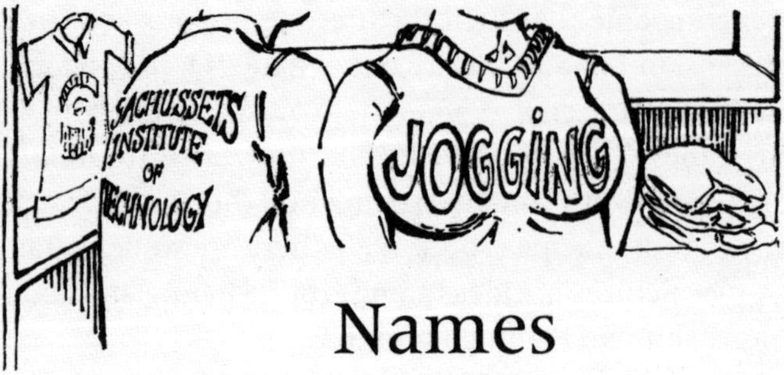

Names

Of course the High Street of the small southern French town where Sophie and I live isn't called the High Street; we just find that a convenient name, for more reasons than you might think. This is the moment to offer a warning to all travellers in France. A surprising number of streets and squares in France have two names: their official one, and the one that people who live there call them by. The French, you see, think that names mean things, and things keep changing, especially in a country which has had more than one revolution and a lot of history, not all of which has been replaced in school by non-élitist creative activities. So French street names get changed, in order to keep up.

This makes the British seem very conservative, or slow on the uptake, or both. Take a French person round London. What is your answer to the question 'Who was Piccadilly? Or was it a battle, or what?' Sorry mate, dunno. 'Downing Street, now – was Downing a famous Prime

Minister?' Ah, um I rather think he was a jobbing builder, but I'm not sure. 'Why don't you call it Churchill Street? We've got a Churchill Street in Paris, and a Franklin Roosevelt Boulevard – why don't you call Grosvenor Square, Roosevelt Square? He's got a statue in the middle . . . Who was Grosvenor anyway?' Oh shut up. Our streets just have names like you and me. They don't *mean* anything.

But deep down the French are just as conservative or slow on the uptake. According to its name-plate, our High Street immortalises a distinguished, heroic and respected local man who became a professor and was done to death in a Nazi concentration camp. And everybody knows that, and is glad that he's got a street named after him. But most people call the street *la rue Nationale,* because it's shorter, and that was what their mums and dads and grandparents always called it. Always? Certainly not. You can bet that any street called *la rue Nationale* – and there are hundreds in France – was called *la rue Royale* until the last royalty was swept aside and the name-plates were rapidly changed.

So if you're going to stay a while in a French town, be just a little sceptical about the town plan that they give you free at the local Tourist Office. If you stand in front of your hotel and ask someone 'What's the name of this street?' it may save getting lost later. The railway station in the town of Tours – and a fine station it is too, all Victorian cast-iron curlicues picked out in bright colours – is in the *Place du Maréchal Leclerc.* So where is the *Place de la Gare,* Station Square, that everyone keeps telling you to go to? Don't go looking for it on the town plan, it's the

Place du Maréchal Leclerc. In Orléans, I'm glad to say, *le pont George Cinq*, the George V bridge, has been George V long enough for everyone to call it that, including – though not very loudly – during the brief unhappy period when it was forced to bear the baleful name-plate *Pont Adolf Hitler*.

Sometimes they leave the old name up as well, if it's nicely carved in the stone. The first time Sophie and I drove to La Rochelle we had a town plan, and we knew that the hotel we'd booked at was just off the *Place de Verdun*. Sophie did the navigating. I said 'Haven't we got to the *Place de Verdun* yet?' 'No,' said Sophie, 'This is the *Place d'Armes*: look, it says so on that building.' We spent the next ten minutes threading through one-way streets in the rush hour and backing out of cul-de-sacs. Dammit, there was the *Place d'Armes* again. Another circuit. Then I asked a policeman. Yes, of course. To go from the *Place d'Armes* to the *Place de Verdun* you just stay where you are.

Which people become streets when they die? If you list them from town plans and leave out abstractions like *Liberté*, *République* and *Paix*, or Peace, the top score goes easily to de Gaulle. His best-known *Place* is round the Arc de Triomphe in Paris, though it's still often called by its previous name, *Place de l'Etoile*. Next comes le maréchal Leclerc, who led his Free French division from Africa to Normandy, bringing them into Paris as the first Allied troops. Third, and not far behind, is Gambetta. He died as long ago as 1882, so he's a long-lasting street name. It was he who got out of Paris by hot-air balloon during the siege in the Franco-Prussian war, but he's a street name because he proclaimed the republic on the 4th September 1870 – and there are a lot of Streets of the 4th September around too. Other common date names are the 8th May, which is VE day, and the 11th November. Dates in June, July and August 1944 show when the town was liberated.

We have a *Boulevard Gambetta* in our town, of course – and an *Avenue Wilson*. That's Woodrow, not Harold, and he keeps a fairly high score; not as high as Voltaire but beating Molière, neither of whom get anywhere near dear old Victor Hugo. We have all three of those writers. I told you this was a very ordinary small town.

If we lower our eyes from the street names we come to the names of the shops. And here's a difference from an English shopping street. Go to an English town that you've never seen before, and you feel at home with familiar shop names, branches of national chains: a well-known cash chemist, a chain shop for books and papers, and branches of national retailers of everything from lamb chops to video cameras. Chains do exist in France. The most noticeable are the chains of mighty hypermarkets: Champion, Mammouth, Casino and others. FNAC is a chain of big bookshops, but you only see those in big towns. Small-town High Street shops have mostly got owners in them, not managers, and they try to be individual even when they're selling stuff manufactured five hundred miles away, or five thousand. For mass-produced factory stuff, the hypermarket just outside our town is a bit cheaper. So is mail order. It's efficiency versus independence and human relations. Efficiency is winning, of course, but still, people here do prefer, if a shop is called Jacques Dupont, to find Jacques Dupont himself behind the counter.

However, opposite Madame Faugerat's chemist's shop there's a shop called Sweatie. It sells clothes to young persons who wish to be up to date and with it: track suits, T-shirts, anoraks in the winter, and that sort of thing, including those odd expensive sports shoes that the French call *baskets*, presumably because they were originally for playing basketball in. For anyone who likes to wear baskets on his feet while shopping, or while playing Space Invaders at the machine in the café near the bus station, Sweatie seems a perfectly good name for that sort of clothes shop. It comes from sweat-shirt, often written – in France anyway – sweet-shirt.

The authorities, including the French Academy and a government department whose sole job is to try to look after the French language, are keen on sweeping back the flood of un-French words threatening their frontiers. *Le week-end* has become, for a lot of people, *la fin de semaine*, and after official prodding *le tour-operator* is sometimes called *le voyagiste*. There is resistance, though. Some years ago hospitals were told to not to call their machine *le scanner* but *le tomodensitomètre*, but it didn't catch on, and I expect you can see why.

Such efforts cut no ice with the young. To be smart, you must have something in a sort of English on your clothes. T-shirts are T-shirts in French, and if you see a T-shirt wearer coming towards you with 'Massachusetts Institute of Technology' written all over his chest, don't go up to him and say 'Ah, how nice to meet a man from

Massachusetts!' At best he will say 'Quoi?' which is French for 'What?' and at worst he'll think you're trying to be rude. And it's not just the young. I can see a bulky lady of a certain age looming up, and she's got the word JOGGING in big letters right across her front. It's exactly the right word too.

Paris may be still a centre of fashion, but cheap leisure clothes have to advertise somewhere like Wyoming or

Chattanooga. Of course they don't come from there. A lot are made in the Far East or elsewhere where labour is cheap, and the English on them is purely decorative. PROTECT WINCH RESERVE, it says in three-inch letters on the back of the girl in front of us. Why and where there is a reserve of winches and why it should need protection is neither here nor there. The pullovers in Sweatie's window can hardly be Authentic Montana University Equipment, though there it is in lavish machine embroidery from neck to waist. I've just discovered that the jeans I bought from a stall in the market are BUILT BY SCIENTISTS. Looking at the small print I see that the scientists concerned are factory-workers on the French island of Martinique, otherwise famous for its rum, and good luck to them. That label is in good English, and tiny and discreet, I'm glad to say. But Sophie bought a bargain-price anorak last winter. A label on the outside, in the middle of her back, proclaimed GUARANTEED GOOD TASTY AND GOOD FEELING. She unpicked that.

Well, to get back to people's names. Did you know that in France you can't simply register your new-born offspring under any first name that pleases your taste and fancy? There's a law about first names: the law of the Eleventh Germinal, Year Two of the Revolution, which allows the French to have only those first names that belong to official saints or persons famous in history. Since then there have been circulars from the Ministry suggesting that registrars should take reasonable note of parents' wishes and even use a prudent amount of common sense. This has allowed foreign first names to creep in – Bryan, Jack, Wolfgang – including some of those odd first names that American film stars have: Rocky and Cindy were recently registered in our Town Hall.

Nevertheless, not so long ago some broadminded parents were frustrated by the *tribunal de grande instance* of Pontoise when they appealed against their registrar's refusal to let their daughter be called Vanille – Vanilla. They claimed it was a nice name, suggestive of refined pleasure. But the tribunal ruled that it would be a handicap to the young person, and likely to provoke mockery. No Vanilla, nor indeed Strawberry or Chocolate. It puts me in a patriotic glow to think that if they had been Britons they would never have been slaves, and could have settled straight away for Raspberry Ripple.

I was looking at the calendar of saints the other day. If you live in France your postman kindly gives you an illustrated calendar every year around Christmas, which naturally provides an opportunity for you to give him a discreet token of appreciation. Each day has its official saint. You need to study the list to know when to give your friends and relations a present on their saint's day, or at least send them a card. So Sophie gets a bunch of flowers on the 25th May, St Sophie's day, which is her *fête*, as well as something on her birthday, her *anniversaire*, and I always hope for breakfast in bed on the 24th June, St John's day. Looking at the calendar, I see that if they had been French my parents could have legally dubbed me Romeo, Nestor, Hyacinth, or Narcissus.

Those are the English forms of official male saints in the French calendar. Perhaps I could get away with being Hyacinth Harris nowadays (the 17th August). In fact it would be useful. The first stuff I wrote for money was a series in a French paper, and 'John Harris' was a delightfully exotic label. But there must be half a million John Harrises in England and America, and I've had to call myself John P. Harris to try to avoid confusion in Grub Street. If I were Hyacinth, now . . . But no. I shudder to think what might have happened at school behind the tuck shop.

On the other hand, French marketing experts can call their products what they like. In our local hypermarket there's a stack of bottles of Edward V whisky – Edward V in English, just like that. When you look at the small print, it turns out to be made in France. Its Scottish rivals boast a hairy-sporraned strength of 44°, but Edward V is a smooth 30°, saving one the trouble of adding water and noticeably reducing the price. It's the name that interests me. No Edward or Edouard ever mounted the French throne. The whisky king must be one of ours, and he's a deserving case too. How kind of the manufacturer to commemorate the elder of the two little princes who were murdered in the Tower. His skeleton is in Westminster Abbey, and now his name is on the lips of hard-up drinkers of French whisky. All's well that ends well, and boo to that horrid Richard III. I believe in Shakespeare, not in the Richard III Society.

But alas! I tried asking a few shoppers 'Who was Edward V?' Thirty per cent were don't knows. The other seventy per cent had in mind Edward VII or George V, both of whom exist dimly but benevolently in the French consciousness, or a vague figure combining both kings, with Edward VII dominating. He is remembered as a jovial stout party when Prince of Wales, living it up in Paris whenever he could get away from his Mama for a bit of *entente cordiale.* I treasure a cutting from France's top daily paper. Back in 1983 it said that a certain beach in Yugoslavia is known as 'the English beach' because it was there that Edward VII swam naked with Mrs Simpson. Yes, Edward VII. That bearded fun-loving king has a strong image among the marketing experts, as well as a few boulevards to his name.

Crime

I've never been mugged yet, nor has my wife Sophie, in England or in France. The only time we've had anything irrecoverably stolen was in 1960, when a thief in Plymouth got a suitcase out of our car. It was full of winter woollies. Average that out, and it comes to less than a square foot of knitwear per year, so far. Not bad.

I suppose we've been lucky. Down here the local paper makes the best of what crime it can get. A fair amount goes on in Montpellier, a big go-ahead town thirty miles from us. Its criminals are mostly young beginners, otherwise unemployed. If they're successful in crime they move on elsewhere. Paris is a fine place for burglars, not up to New York standards, but as good as London. The Riviera offers opportunities for all kinds of crook. The late Mr Graham Greene lived there, and got into trouble a few years ago when he wrote a pamphlet about the local mafia. It was banned in France as libellous, largely at the instigation of Monsieur Jacques

Médecin. He had been Mayor of Nice for ages, like his father before him. He suggested that Mr Greene was out for publicity, a thing Monsieur Médecin had never been afraid of himself – until, and nothing to do with Mr Greene, he got his comeuppance. He's now in South America, with a prison sentence waiting for him if he returns.

Down our way, in this obscure part of Languedoc, there are few pickings. Crooks do better in favoured rural areas of Provence. They even caught a highwayman there last year. There were forty hold-ups and twenty rapes on his balance-sheet, and they hope to pin the murder of a couple of German tourists on him as well.

If you're a workaholic criminal like that, you go to the Big City out of the tourist season. But if you want a quiet winter in the country, with modest takings and no risk, you track down one of those farmhouses that have been ever so tastefully converted by rich persons from Paris or Copenhagen or Basingstoke. Keep your eye open for activities in the local plumbing trade. If jacuzzis are being installed, and a fancy-shaped swimming-pool, and state-of-the-art oil heating in case the chap wants to come down at Christmas, you're all right if this idyllic pad is suitably private. It probably will be. Your average rich persons don't want to be seen from the road or by neighbours as they bask on their terrace sipping their champagne and toying with their foie-gras-and-truffle sandwiches.

When he has locked up and disappeared northwards, bronzed and fat, you can park your lorry in his shrubbery and get to work at leisure. Don't bother with the expensive burglar-proof doors or shutters. Unpack your ladder and get up on the roof. Remove some tiles and slither down your climbing-rope. Or start on a likely wall with a battering-ram. At worst you'll get a video-recorder and a lot of copper piping. You might find some local antique furniture or pottery which will find a buyer next tourist season. A friend of ours has a holiday house deep in a wood in Provence, near – but well out of sight of – Alphonse Daudet's celebrated windmill. He bought some old oak doors, carved with heraldic animals and subjects from classical mythology, and adapted the inside of his house to fit them. Out they went one November, through a jagged hole in the wall, and a grateful wild boar and his harem settled in for the winter. That is the price of privacy in fashionable parts.

Areas like that have long been deserted by the natural population, unless they've turned themselves into jobbing builders catering for transient foreigners' whims. Burglars drive around making careful notes, people instal electronic alarms, and it's getting like the Chilterns or the Cotswolds.

Fortunately there are still areas where ordinary people go on living and dying, working and spending some of their free time on keeping up to date on the neighbours. Nobody buys burglar alarms in the villages round here. Of course you can't have everything. If a stranger wanders through a working village he feels that behind every shutter there's a beady eye on him, and an attentive granny wondering what he's up to. And he's dead right. We do have summer people, who own village

houses or rent them furnished, but they are rapidly analysed, discussed and classified as assets or liabilities, or just harmless. They soon learn how important it is to keep the population informed.

Long ago, when we were settling into our previous house in the village, we had some English friends to stay. They're a married couple, both doctors. I asked our local doctor to look in for a drink when he was next in the village. So we all had an agitated discussion about the National Health systems of our two countries, and Dr Tessier's well-known car spent an hour and a half in the square. The village was worried. I found that I had a lot of explaining to do, as I went for my evening walk. No, I was quite all right. And Sophie, who had seemed so full of beans in the morning at the travelling grocer's, was still full of beans. So were our hitherto unidentified guests. It was Sophie's fault. The queue at the grocer's van is where to put people in the picture.

We learnt our lesson. Village gossip must be hell if you've got something to hide, but it's a pretty good security system.

It reminds me of that splendid bit near the beginning of Marcel Proust's great novel. The narrator's aunt is confined to her room. She sees an unknown dog trotting down the street, and Madame Imbert carrying some unusually good-looking asparagus; and she hears Dr Piperaud's doorbell. She summons Françoise, the cook, who is given no peace until the two of them have provisionally identified the dog and the garden that the asparagus came from. Then Françoise can go and find out who had been to the doctor.

Village human nature hasn't changed much since Proust's time. If you don't want to be burgled, live somewhere where they notice the asparagus you're bringing home. Especially in France. Over a hundred years ago John Stuart Mill wrote about 'the contrast between the frank sociability and amiability of French personal intercourse, and the English mode of existence in which everybody acts as if everybody else . . . was either an enemy or a bore.' Of course a lot of English people did think Mill was an enemy or a bore, with all his alarming notions – votes for women indeed! – but in France he was just the local Englishman. Sociability and all that, including inquisitiveness, keeps down crime, especially where it's dry and sunny three hundred days a year, with elderly villagers keeping an eye on things from strategically located benches. If you parked your GB car somewhere in the village we used to live in, I would have been given your description before nightfall.

So you can see what a shock was caused by the Great Pumpkin Robbery. I used to have one of the village allotments, down by the spring. Ten years ago my wife Sophie and I were tending a pumpkin. Not that we're keen on eating pumpkins – nor are the French either, really, but it's traditional to make pumpkin soup once or twice in the winter, when you can see pumpkins on market stalls, being sold in big golden-yellow slices at a few francs a kilo. Pumpkins are magnificent to look at, gratifying to grow, and terribly romantic, what with Cinderella, who was really a French girl called Cendrillon, and Halloween, and all that. We thought that we would try to outdo our fellow allotmenteers for once. We had bought a packet of seeds in Italy. The Zucca Verruca di Chioggia, according to the packet, was going to be enormous, deep yellow and covered all over with longitudinal furrows and mighty warts.

The seeds germinated eagerly. We selected the best plant for lavish treatment. There's a pseudo-ranch not far away, where tourists can hire horses. I had a deux-chevaux car in those days, ideal for transporting the horse's valuable product, and the ranch-owner kindly let me help myself when I turned up with a spade and a plastic sack. I made a mound of this nutritious stuff, and dug a trench all round, leading to my main watering-trench. (We water by irrigation down here, opening and closing channels with a wide heavy hoe.) Three times a week, at dawn, I filled the moat. And the plant responded as though it knew it had to produce the biggest and ugliest pumpkin in the village: hairy leaves appeared, and thick stems that soon grew: three feet, six feet, and longer. And then flowers, large and coarse. And at last, a baby. I suppressed all the subsequent babies: this one was going to be a spoilt only child. I measured it daily, with a piece of string.

It responded beautifully. Soon I was giving it a long drink every morning; and a stroke and a little talk. At last its growth-rate slowed down, and it began to change colour from green to orange. Its skin became rough and hard. Puberty; soon it would come of age. I reckoned it would weigh in at about twenty-five pounds. That's by no means a record for pumpkins, but we loved it all the same. And my allotment neighbours, a competitive band, proud of their aubergines and canteloupe melons, who in the last couple of years had watched, criticized and encouraged my attempts at learning the differences between, on the one hand, gardening under the mild moist influence of the Gulf Stream with its kindly drizzle and diffused light, and on the other hand bending the back in the Mediterranean glare – they were kind enough to admire our warty offspring.

At sunset on the 30th September our pumpkin was

looking happy and fit. By breakfast time on the 1st October it had disappeared.

This was not so much a loss as an embarrassment. A pumpkin, even a twenty-five-pounder, isn't worth much, but the news caused consternation among the village gardeners, who started counting their tomatoes, and among the rest of the village, up to and including Monsieur Delmas the Mayor.

One doesn't want suspicion and dissension in a small village where everybody knows everybody. There had been, shortly after we came, the case of Monsieur and Madame Ferrand. They were Parisians. He was a retired policeman. That wasn't a point in his favour. Policemen aren't terribly popular in rural France, and the village gets on very well without them. And anyway a French mayor is automatically an Officer of Justice. Perhaps part of the prejudice goes back to the war years, when the police had to do more or less what the Occupying Germans told them – until a week or two before the liberation, when most of them downed tools and joined the resistance. Madame Ferrand was the real problem. As a Parisienne she always knew best – about cooking, and what to buy and what not to buy from the vans of the travelling tradesmen who set up shop twice a week in the square, and how to bring up children and whether the doctor had prescribed the right medicines. The crisis came when her cat disappeared. She was righteously indignant, and suggested that someone from the village might have eaten it – probably one of the Spaniards. Now our so-called Spaniards are nice people and well integrated. The old ones are veterans of the anti-Franco side in the Spanish Civil War, from Catalonia, a hundred and fifty miles west, and the others are their children – not Spaniards at all but French, although they have names like Gomez and Martinez and Garcia. The Ferrands were regarded as outsiders, but the Spaniards aren't. That annoyed Madame Ferrand, but the accusation of cat-eating annoyed the village even more.

She told us that she didn't suspect us, because it's well known that the English are sentimental about cats and even about things that good Parisians eat, like horses and snails. Oddly enough my wife Sophie *has* eaten cat. That was in early 1945, when she was a schoolgirl in the part of Holland that was still occupied by the SS, and people really were dying of hunger. Cat was known as roof rabbit in those days, and fetched a high price on the black market – not surprisingly, as all there was on the rations was sugar-beet residue after the sugar had been extracted from it.

Anyhow, after Madame Ferrand's unjust accusation had got around, hardly anyone would speak to the Ferrands, and soon afterwards they sold their house and are now said to be spending their retirement somewhere up in the Frozen North near Orléans.

So you can see why I was embarrassed. I agreed, loudly and often, that it couldn't be someone from the village. It takes a long while to eat one's way through a twenty-five-pound pumpkin, and during the process the news would be bound to leak out. It must have been someone from outside, with a car to take the thing away in. Probably a *chasseur*, that is to say someone with a shot-gun, who had come near the village in the early morning to try for a pheasant or a thrush or two and hadn't wanted to go home empty-handed.

Wednesdays are market days in the nearest town. Week by week I inspected the pumpkins there. But no, none resembled ours. I knew each wart and wrinkle of our offspring. And anyway I'd scratched my initials on it when it was young, and Sophie had scratched hers, which is one of the charming things about pumpkins: you can watch the tattoo grow . . .

On the 1st November, exactly one month after the great robbery, I went down to harvest the last of the sweet peppers. And there was my pumpkin, exactly where it had been, intact, unharmed. If only it could have talked, to say what had happened and what conversations it had heard! A mystery. Nobody in the village could offer an intelligent suggestion to explain it, though they seemed pleased at this happy ending. If it had been England I would have suspected that someone had borrowed it for a competition at a flower show, but they don't go in for such exhibitionism down here. Perhaps the thief had been joyful at first, then worried, then remorseful and anxious, and had gone to confession – and the priest had told him to make restitution as the price of absolution. It's possible, just, though pumpkin-stealing can be only a venial sin, hardly a mortal one.

The mystery of the kidnapped pumpkin has never been solved.

Cross my heart, it really happened.

TRYING TO AMUSE THE FRENCH

In the early eighties I wrote about fifty pieces for *Le Monde-Dimanche,* a Sunday supplement of *Le Monde. Le Monde* is a fanatically serious paper, but its Sunday supplement was more relaxed (and was eventually abolished).

I enjoy writing in French. It takes me three times as long as writing in English, but producing a usable sentence in that trickily elegant language makes me feel like an apprentice tightrope walker (*un funambuliste* – what a nice word) who has fried his first egg thirty feet up. And there is the magpie satisfaction, when reading a novel or a newspaper or a dictionary – anything from Rabelais to the day's horoscope – of finding an interesting word and pinching it for myself. Sometimes I angled a paragraph or a whole article to get it in. Perhaps only a foreigner can feel like that about a language.

I made mistakes, an average of one per article, and a kind subeditor corrected them. For example, I usually double-check genders, but I didn't bother with *dynamo*. It looks so masculine. Amazement: my *son dynamo* (about Sophie's father, who spent wartime evenings in his Amsterdam attic pedalling to hear the BBC) appeared as *sa dynamo*. I couldn't believe it. But the dictionary – all the dictionaries – said that the subeditor was right. (It's feminine in most other languages too, I discovered, even in Russian with those tough-kneed Moscow Dynamos.) French without tears, and a cheque too.

About half my *Le Monde* pieces were set in the fictional village of Saint-Fulcran-de-Fobis – Saint-Fulcran for short. I have little imagination, so Saint-Fulcran bears a strong resemblance to the village Sophie and I were living in. Fulcran was the Christian name of its oldest male inhabitant. St Fulcran himself was a very capable tenth-century bishop of Lodève.

I have translated and messed about with the following pieces with that glorious freedom that comes from knowing that the original writer cannot protest. Interpolations for this book are in square brackets.

Screams in the square

DURING working hours I am usually the only male person over two years old at home in the square. Most of the female persons in Saint-Fulcran are sexist. They think in terms of ladies and gentlemen when it's a question of who should deal with emergencies. When the hubbub broke out I was next door at Madame Vidal's on top of her kitchen table, fitting in a light bulb. Earlier that morning she had commissioned me to buy her one in town, catching me as I was getting the car out.

'A 220 watt bulb.'

'Are you sure it's 220 watts, Madame? Screw or bayonet?'

'Euh . . . perhaps it's 110 . . . or six. Come and see.'

Although I'm not sure myself how many amps make an ohm or whether the volts go from negative to positive in Australia like water down plug-holes, I can identify and change light bulbs with masculine bravado. Madame Vidal is rightly afraid of electricity and always asks me to do the dangerous work when her torch needs a new battery.

So there I was, up among the fly-papers, when the

brouhaha began. Descending with care via one of Madame Vidal's kitchen chairs (contemporary with their owner, eighty-plus, but less robust), I joined her behind the lace curtains.

It was the aliens, trapped in their Volvo. Intermittently racing in neutral, its motor was making a good deal of noise. So were Mesdames Mazel and Bezombes.

The aliens had arrived on Sunday. People aren't inquisitive in Saint-Fulcran, but we do take an interest, especially when an unknown couple rents a *gîte rural*, a holiday cottage, in mid-winter. The Volvo had a DK roundel on it, but it also bore the label of a car-hire company. We soon learned that they weren't Danes, because Madame Bec once had a Norwegian boy friend. She owns the *gîte*, and reported that the language they used to each other wasn't Scandinavian. She had to settle them in with sign-language, because they didn't speak French. Queer.

They had a big black Labrador with them. It seemed sociable, especially towards Toutone, Monsieur Gal's female gun-mongrel. But the aliens kept their distance, going out in their hired Volvo at breakfast time and coming back at nightfall. Their language was unidentifiable, despite every discreet effort at overhearing. White; in their sixties; she was tall and grumpy-looking; he, medium-sized and depressed.

Early on the previous evening there had been a small explosion in their *gîte*. Then they had come out on to the square and driven off somewhere, with the Labrador. Black smoke was coming from the open door. Madame Bec's son went in, and soon got the incident under control. It was the sort of awkwardness that can happen with the fuel-oil heater in the Bec *gîte*: if tenants don't understand that you must turn off the feed-tap firmly before going out for the day, a pool of oil can collect, leading to trouble if you try to light the thing regardless. That prelude to the happening had provided an interesting distraction for the citizens gathered in the square.

Leaving my place of safety behind Madame Vidal's curtains, I went out. My wife Sophie put me in the picture. While I was in town the aliens had returned. The lady shouted and jumped up and down. Madame Bec fetched Sophie in the hope that she might be able to act as interpreter, if the aliens could speak English. The lady could indeed – with force if not with accuracy. Sophie was to tell Madame Bec and the villagers – half a dozen were lending an ear – that Saint-Fulcran was a dump; that the oil-heater was a public danger and probably booby-trapped; that they had spent the night in a hotel in town and the poor Labrador had been so upset that he had kept them awake until dawn; that Languedocians were no better than they ought to be and the inhabitants of Saint-Fulcran the very bottom; and that they were going to be off without wasting a further moment.

The husband silently hastened to load the car and got into the driving seat. The lady uttered a few more sharp judgements that Sophie thought better not to translate, made an imperious gesture towards the north . . . and zoom!

The northern exit from the square is wide enough for a car, for at least five yards. Then, deceptively, it bends north-east and becomes a pedestrian-sized tunnel under

Monsieur Gal's house. Trying to back out of this vehicular dead end, the husband had apparently scored a groove on a green-painted oil-drum, the property of Madame Mazel and the home of her beloved oleander. She complained. He got out and made vague apologetic gestures; got in again; reversed awkwardly and jammed a rear hub-cap against the bottom step of the stone staircase that leads to Madame Bezombes' front door. Pélagie Bezombes was there, and giving tongue. Her shrieks were well-intentioned, because if the husband were to manage to continue reversing in more or less the same direction, his rear wheel would drop down some fifteen inches into the space leading to Madame Bezombes' cellar, and a fork-lift tractor or something like that would be needed to get him out. The husband's nerve seemed to have snapped and he was getting his pedals mixed up. The wife had got out. Pélagie Bezombes' normal voice is piercing. The wife had presumably caught and misunderstood the word *putain*. In village speech it is a simple intensifier: *cette putain de marche* – that wretched step – but basically it means a female of easy virtue. The wife must have caught this word – perhaps there is a cognate word in her own mysterious language – and was reacting briskly. Then she ordered her quivering husband out of the car.

At this point people noticed me, an apparently able-bodied non-quivering male. I was hustled into the driving seat. Tentatively, forwards like a tortoise and backwards like a lobster, I edged the car out into the square. Then I changed places with the husband. I had begun to quiver a bit myself.

Off they went, down the steep alley in front of our house; and stopped again, because their off-side front wheel had entered Madame Vidal's door. It was luckily open, and Madame Vidal had jumped aside like a matador.

The wife once more ejected her tearful husband, and gestured for me. I obeyed. As I drove the car to the road outside the village the Labrador growled.

After they had gone I needed a stiff cognac. There are times when I regret that English has become such an international language.

Next day Madame Mazel told us: 'I couldn't sleep a wink last night after all that, but dear me! I wouldn't have missed it for worlds.'

Le Monde, 21st February 1982

Imperialisms

WINTER is when we smugly say 'How clever to live in the Midi!' Nordic persons, once swishing yellow hair above mahogany torsos, are now toiling pallidly in fog. Parisian noses are at the grindstone. Classrooms and homework keep local youth and its minders out of mischief. At this time of year Baudelaire shuddered at the funereal thud of logs being dumped on the cobbles of his courtyard, and pinched Longfellow's muffled drums for a gloomy poem of his own. But Paul Valéry in his *cimetière marin*, a few miles south from here at Sète, could have basked today. I'm all right too. I come out to my *cagnard* like a lizard.

A *cagnard* is a sunny nook sheltered from wind. Not our back yard, where a northerly breeze is whirling. But in front of our front door, which is up a flight of steps from the road, there is just room for a deck chair. Until lunchtime, when the sun will go round the corner behind Madame Vidal's house, one can purr in the sun.

Here I am and here I hope to stay, with my Rubik's cube and a glass of clairette. I can hear the mason on the roof of the church (it's next door, we have a party wall). He's whistling a familiar tune. I whistle in descant.

'*Té*!' he says. 'You know that?'

'Of course. It's called "Colonel Bogey".'

'Oh no no. It's very well known. It's "The Bridge on the River Kwaï".'

French imperialism seems boundless. That French novel by Pierre Boulle, which inspired the film, isn't bad. But 'Colonel Bogey' was flourishing in England half a century before the Burma railroad.

'Listen, I'll teach you the words that cheered the Eighth Army in the desert, when they weren't singing "Lili Marlene":

Hitler
Has only got one ball.
Goering
Has two, but very small.
Himmler
Is somewhat similar,
And Goebbels has no balls at all.'

Back on his roof the mason sings happily. He's a bright pupil: he took only ten minutes to learn the words. A mason's time is almost as valuable as a plumber's. [Those rude words were in English on the roof – and in the paper, where "the decent obscurity of a learned language" confers respectability.]

Discovering that 'Colonel Bogey' has been naturalized as *Le Pont sur la rivière Kwaï* reminds me of another example of linguistic imperialism. The other week I went to town to see – at last – *2001, A Space Odyssey*. Of course it was dubbed into French. An astronaut arrives at the space station. For de-briefing, he faces a supercomputer. There are a dozen buttons, so that he can choose his language: English, Chinese, French, Russian. . . . He firmly presses the button marked 'English', and at once a voice asks him: *'Quelle est votre nationalité?'* Without blinking an eyelid this able man replies: *'Américaine.'* Bravo for him, but I could see that things would soon go wrong, with gremlins like that in their whatsit. Sabotage by an engineer from Quebec, perhaps?

The front door opens behind me.

'What are you up to?'

'I'm trying to do this damn cube before lunch, but – '

'At your age! And where everyone can see you!'

I see what's on her mind. On the 29th October there was a highly interesting article in *Le Monde*, on Rubik's cube. I was looking at it this morning, and Sophie must have seen it on my desk, with its headline: THIS OBSCURE OBJECT OF DESIRE and the sub-title EROTIC PLEASURE. She will have read that *you hold it in your hand like a woman's breast*, and that it fills the user with *a masturbatory pleasure . . .*

'My dear, the French themselves say that they can compensate for not having oil wells by having bright ideas instead. Rubik is Hungarian, but they want this cube to glow with the lights of Gay Paree, perhaps of the *Place Pigalle*. I grew up in the light reflected from the screen by Mae West, and if you think that a cube measuring 5.7 cm and weighing less than 100 grammes. . . . Anyway, if I'm obsessed by problems in three dimensions and six colours I don't see how. . . .'

'Men are all alike, whether they're French or English. Give me your cube and go and chop some firewood.'

I obey. She sits down.

It's a fact that there isn't room for two in this *cagnard*. The logs thud in our courtyard. As I chop I sing 'Colonel Bogey'.

Le Monde, 10th January 1981

Windows

DEAR Fred,

Congratulations! I've just had your letter from Basingstoke. So at last you've bought your dream house! An unspoilable view, an acre of wild shrubs, three and a half walls and most of the roof in working order; and the possibility of negotiating for electricity, all thanks to a kindly Languedocian who is drying his tears in a modern council flat.

Now you can look forward to holidays devoted to the joys and triumphs of *le do-it-yourself*. I'll answer your questions later, about plumbers, doctors (yes, bring your own thermometer, or else . . .) and the Mairie. Windows, first. You really ought to bring a couple from England.

Think for a moment of the good British window-sill. Long ago blue-eyed virgins sat there like damsels at castle turrets, hoping for the postman and a letter in a beloved hand from some outpost: the North-West Frontier, the Limpopo, Menton . . . More prosaically, it's where we kept the telephone when Sophie and I lived in Cornwall; if she opened the window I could take calls without having to come in and take off my gum-boots. That was where the cat sat on her cushion, keeping an eye on things among the wintering potted plants. Magic casements opening on the foam, or on what-have-you.

Of course in sober fact half of the window space isn't made to open at all, and the magic casement when open to its maximum is merely ajar, with an ingenious hinged metal whatsit to keep it that way. The magic is the window-sill.

Well, as far as I can judge from your description of the house, you'll have to be buying new window frames from the builders' merchant. When you do, you'll come to grips with the astounding fact that there are no window-sills in French houses. Not in French *rooms*, that is. The window-sills are on the outside. The cat sitting there is out in the open, looking in: perhaps a stranger, an enemy tom on the prowl.

Windows here open inwards. The practical natives sacrifice indoor window-sills so that they can open their windows into the room, and clean them themselves. The Amalgamated Society of British Window Cleaners would never allow that. There are no window cleaners in France – no breezy chaps with ladder, bucket and chamois leather; no jokes about what they see and whom they pleasure, no old music-hall songs . . . A whole branch of folk-lore missing. The French have to make do with stories about chimney-sweeps.

On the outdoor side of the window-sill they have shutters. The first thing a French child says in England is: 'What, no shutters?' The French use shutters instead of heavy opaque curtains. They close them every night and open them every morning, having first opened (inwards) their windows to do the job. The shutters open outwards, like British windows. You can't have both, if you follow me. Tell the French child about the ASBWC and the strikes it would call if our island race started putting in his parents' sort of window.

So if you want your pussycat to snooze on the sill between the boxes of tomato seedlings, with velvet curtains keeping the world out, bring the window-frames with you. Mind you, you can't have them on the ground floor. Your insurance policy will say that if you go away for more than twenty-four hours you must shut the shutters downstairs, or get nothing back if a burglar calls. To transform idle theft into proper breaking-and-entering, something better than glass is needed. Of course, iron bars not more than twelve centimetres apart will do, but you wouldn't like that. No, for the best of both worlds have the French sort downstairs, wide wide open when it's nice outside, and close the shutters when the sun's too hot. Then when the wind and the rain are lashing, you can go upstairs to your English lair, put the teapot on the window-sill and settle down with the latest parcel of Penguins or the World Service. You can buy the ladder and the chamois leather over here.

Why, by the way, do you sometimes get rained on in a narrow French alley on a dry day? Because if an upper-floor window opens the French way, you can string a little washing-line outside, a few inches from the wall. Drip, drip.

Le Monde, 8th March 1981

Spit, please

WHAT about dentists?

Generalizations about national character spring luxuriant from fragmentary data. Over the years a score of British dentists have drudged between my jaws, but only one Frenchman. The sample is small, but that won't stop me: art is long but life is short, and before I can make a tour of representative French dentists' chairs I shall have no teeth left to speak of.

Stories about dentists [have you read V.S. Pritchett?] are an impressive branch of English folklore. France is disappointing. In my struggles to understand the French soul I always keep Hervé Nègre's *Dictionnaire des Histoires Drôles* by my bedside. It contains only two funny stories about dentists, as compared with ninety-three about the clergy, sixty-nine about doctors, forty-two about the English and seven about hippopotami. Obviously the fee-fie-fo-fum element is lacking.

Now I know why.

When you lose a filling in England, unless you go to a dental hospital (a good solution if you don't mind being an exhibit for a squad of cheery students), you wait three or four weeks with ambivalent emotions until you open wide before a NHS dentist. Then it's on with the job. Disagreeable needles in the gums, in case the dentist thinks your grunts or writhings might be a nuisance; five minutes' boring into the guilty tooth; impromptu drilling into other teeth while he's at it; a bit of amalgam –

'What did you think of the Spurs–Arsenal match?'

'Aargh!'

'No, nor did I. Spit. Next, please!'

While with Dr Caramel . . .

General conversation first. We aren't in a hurry, oh no. Caramel is a sensitive man, an artist. (British dentists are former rugby players.) We are both almost debonair. If he were a cause of pain he would be stricken with remorse until nightfall and beyond. Three minutes in the chair is as long as a reasonable man can put up with, he seems to think; and then a week off until we meet again.

'Ah yes, you're right, you've lost a filling.'

'Will you have to pull it out?'

'Heavens, what an idea! Let's take a little X-ray . . .'

A week later, Caramel sorrowfully announces that the tooth is alive. British dentists prefer live teeth. Live teeth give you toothache, regularly, throughout your life, and so you come to the surgery in the proper state for a patient, in anguish and ready for anything; they can bore their holes right, left and centre until at last a tooth becomes unprofitable and grumpily they root it out. But

Caramel prefers dead teeth.

'A little *nécro*, please, Mademoiselle. . . . There we are. Next week, same day, same time?'

Three more appointments and the tooth is dead. Caramel can sculpt away without fear of a negative reaction.

But I have disappointed him. He would love to give me a beautiful gold crown to delight anyone gazing down into the depths with the aid of a little mirror on a stick. Terribly sorry, but I've heard that in France one can get stainless steel teeth. I'd always thought they were reserved for officers of the KGB. If one day I have several I might be able to open beer-bottles with them, like Marlon Brando in that film . . . [The point here is that the French NHS refunds almost the whole cost of a stainless steel crown, but gives not a centime more if you want your crown golden or white; those colours therefore cost the patient a bomb. Caramel refuses stainless steel for front teeth, but can be persuaded for molars.]

Caramel gives way.

Week after week he sculpts, takes impressions, and tries the model out . . .

At last the job is done. Using a pocket torch Sophie admires it. But something is lacking. British dentists have punctuated my life with sensational happenings. With Dr Caramel it's just a halt in the shopping.

Patience et longueur de temps
Font plus que force ni que rage.

Where has the drama gone?

Le Monde, 4th December 1983

The milieu

[ALAS, how this piece dates! Time, like an ever-rolling stream, bears all its sons away . . . Graham Greene and Laurence Durrell are no more and the ex-Mayor of Nice, Monsieur Jacques Médecin, is, as I mentioned before, on the run in South America. But I am proud of dragging in my sole contribution to literary criticism, the discovery of a Greenian sub-text. It produced no stir among the French intelligentsia . . . Better luck this time?]

When that very important person the Mayor of Nice (his name escapes me) accuses the world's best living novelist of acting for the sake of mere self-advertisement, one can't help suspecting a certain amount of understandable jealousy. Graham Greene has suggested that corruption and banditism seem to benefit from fellow-feeling in high places, over there at his end of the Mediterranean coast, and I will pluck up my courage to squeak a feeble echo from this corner.

Saint-Fulcran is a long way from the Riviera. Sixty years ago, when living was cheap if you had pounds or dollars, you couldn't go out between Toulon and Nice without bumping into a Huxley, a Fitzgerald, a Mansfield, a Maugham or the luck of the draw from Bloomsbury. Now there's only the author of *The Power and the Glory*. Houses and dinners cost less as one pushes south-west. Beyond Laurence Durrell's stamping-ground in the Gard, Saint-Fulcran lurks in the sticks.

And if Monsieur Delmas, the mayor of this obscure commune, accuses me of evoking certain suspicious local goings-on in the hope of seeing my name in print in a Sunday paper, well, perhaps he's not as mistaken as his opposite number in Nice.

But to return to Greene for a moment. I have been an addict of his since *Brighton Rock*, before the war, when I was fifteen. At the risk of seeming frivolous I will confess a secondary reason for my Greenophily: I am a sucker for sweets, and I suspect Greene of the same weakness. Brighton rock itself: does the average Frenchman know that it isn't part of the coastline? In *The Ministry of Fear*, where do the enemy agents hide their secrets? In a dark rich fruit cake, in the days of strict sugar rationing. Then there are those Maltesers; Greene crunched them when he was a film critic, and they play a key rôle in *The Human Factor* . . . The sweet tooth shows itself in minor details. In *Travels with my Aunt*, the angels on that aunt's buffet have robes striped like peppermint rock, and the narrator's hobby is jam-making. 'I loved chocolate once. I am growing old,' says Aunt Augusta, and we wish a long youth to Greene at Antibes, between the marzipan calissons of Aix and the crystallized fruits of Nice. The blitzed newspaper in *The End of the Affair* relates the Commons debate on sweet rationing, and the unfortunate hero of *Dr Fischer of Geneva* works in a chocolate factory. . .

Good and evil: the sinister chief medical officer of the Intelligence Service poisons an innocent man with *salted* peanuts in *The Human Factor*. In *Ways of Escape* we learn that the real doctor, a kindly inefficient man, didn't want

Greene posted to Sierra Leone and diagnosed diabetes. Greene went to see a specialist: he found instead 'a small sugar deficiency'. One might have guessed. I look forward to seeing a thesis from Texas: *The Sweet and the Sour: confectionery in the works of Graham Greene.*

To get back to Saint-Fulcran. Judge for yourself:

1 There was the mysterious affair of the kidnapping of my beloved pumpkin (see page 67). It was never cleared up. Was it an obscure warning?

2 At the last village bingo night there were fifteen games and sixty-four players.

a) Monsieur Delmas called the numbers until half-time. Madame Carivenc won a *panier garni* containing a guinea fowl, a saucisson, a giant can of cassoulet, a bottle of champagne and a box of chocolates.

b) Monsieur Bouladou, the deputy mayor with sergeant-major's larynx, then took over (with tasteless jests when 20, 69 and 88 came up). And who is his sister? Madame Carivenc! And who won the hamper of oysters? Madame Combadazou, née Delmas!

c) And what did I win? Nothing.

3 Three weeks ago I started keeping chickens, and their maize started disappearing. I put down a British mousetrap, the sort with a strong spring. The next day the mousetrap had gone. So I bought a French mousetrap with three holes (one for an intelligent mouse, one for a slow-witted mouse and one for a real Charlie). Result: another mousetrap gone, and *OCorico* spray-canned on the hen-roost.

I am taking my precautions.

Le Monde, 4th April 1982

[Attempts at humour are better left untranslated. However, in reference to the graffito above: *cocorico* is the French for cock-a-doodle-do, and is also, roughly, the French reply to 'St George for England!' OC is what enthusiasts for Occitanian independence like to spray on surfaces. The incident is purely imaginary; I have never had any chickens or graffiti. As for the numbers, 88 can pass: Brigitte Bardot and Jeanne Moreau. Out of date even in 1982, but it's a backward village.]

Emotion

IMPORTANT: PERSONAL DOCUMENTS it says on the thick envelope. All agog (residence permit? extradition?) I tear it open. An impeccably typed letter:

> Dear Monsieur John Harris,
> This is to inform you that you may soon be able to claim no less than 150000 francs in CASH . . . In which case, at 9.30 a.m. precisely on the first of June 1981 an armoured security van will leave the BNP bank at Bagneux for the HARRIS house – unless you would prefer to receive a cheque made out to Monsieur JOHN HARRIS. . . .

All I have to do, I see, is to send back the certificates that already have my name in capitals on the top, after writing on them the two (two!) personal numbers that I will find on another of the enclosed certificates. Splendid! Quick, quick! There's another certificate, but that merely gives me fifty per cent off a year's subscription to a monthly of no interest. [It's Sélection, the French version of Readers' Digest.] That goes in the wastepaper basket. Ah! In a little wrapper there's a key made of something like aluminium foil. If I enclose that, I shall get not 150 000 francs but 250 000!

Looking through this batch of documents more carefully I note that there are 9999 other prizes, including a thousand games of *touché-coulé*. [Research in the dictionary suggests that *touché-coulé* is a tarted-up version of battleships, which we used to play at school on squared paper when the teacher wasn't watching.] Thanks, but I'd rather see that armoured vehicle turning into the square.

Am I wrong to disdain the monthly? *You will discover the hidden facets of your personality: recently there was a series on the biological and psychological bases of amorous behaviour* . . . Dear me, no. Let those facets remain hidden.

I invest in a stamp, and trot across the square to the letter-box, purring with satisfaction. Appearing from time to time in *Le Monde* seems to pay. People have heard of me! The President hasn't invited me yet to a garden party at the Elysée Palace, but this is a start. How lucky I am not to have died young like Keats!

Hullo, here's Madame Combadazou. She's going to the box with the same envelope. That's funny. She's a tower of strength in her husband's vineyards, and bright with it, but has she been sending in hopeful freelance articles to the Paris press? Unlikely. And there's Madame Pons coming too . . .

We sit on the bench under the mulberry tree to sort it out. Why have we been selected by this benevolent organization? We examine our biographies.

It's a come-down. All three of us have been buying cheap clothes from a mail-order firm; and mailing lists can be sold.

Perhaps we'll have a *touché-coulé* match one day.

Le Monde, 22nd March 1981

Testing, testing

I'VE been away from Saint-Fulcran, doing a week's examining in spoken English in a big town. Sophie came with me, less to counterbalance the charms of female graduate students of Business Administration than to *faire du shopping* with the profits from this trip. The bottom line: she is ten years younger (hairdresser, *visagiste*, latest summer fashions); I am ten years older.

The French are optimists. They think they can make an Englishman work for more than an hour and a half without a tea-break. Even under Madame Thatcher, methodical sipping of the tranquilliser punctuates toil at conveyor belts and Number Ten. In the desert Monty and the Eighth Army kept going from Alamein to Tunis by stopping for elevenses and at 4.30, digging little holes in the sand, pouring in a pint of petrol and calmly brewing up.

Optimists and merciless. I have come through, but it was tough. From eight in the morning until six in the evening, with only a couple of hours in the middle for a four-course break, the anxious candidates kept coming. I try for Buddha-like detachment, but I can't help empathizing. This young man sweats, and I have to mop my brow. The neck of that young lady gradually develops red patches, and I begin to scratch. I try to radiate the cheery kindliness of Father Christmas, but I know that for them I am Jehovah on Judgement Day, or Satan enthroned in the torture chamber. So how on earth can they be expected to natter to me fluently and gracefully, or even comprehensibly, in what the French persist in calling the language of Shakespeare?

Am I too mean with my marks? Here's this luscious creature flashing her eyes, lips and décolleté at me – have I decided to fail her just to prove my objectivity? Or is that sexism on my part; leaning over backwards? This young man who is going at it nineteen to the dozen – is it in an unknown tongue or has my attention drifted away to the clock?

On the other hand, am I too indulgent? I have lived so long with a foot in each of two countries that French English has lost much of its mystery. If a moderately anglophone Frenchman tells me that he is leaving on a sheep I know at once that he's living on a ship, and when he talks of arrears I can see if he means areas. Should he pass? If he were Japanese, would he fail because I've never studied Japanese English? Poor Japanese – and they commit suicide with such alacrity . . . Wake up! The nineteen-to-the-dozen fellow is still at it.

Back at the hotel I admire Sophie's purchases of the day. I am only half listening to her adventures. She was born and raised in Amsterdam. Would I give her twenty out of twenty for English? Nobody gets twenty. Nineteen? But she is faultless, impeccable, whereas I have become deaf, mute and prosopagnosic*, and am worth hardly a charitable seven.

* I found (and bagged for use one day) the word *prosopagnosie* in *Le Monde* four years ago. It means the inability to recognize faces – a rare symptom, except in weary examiners consulting the trombinoscope of the year.

How peaceful it is at Saint-Fulcran! But even in this little vineyard village some English gets 'done'. Not, happily, at the exalted business level where I have to bone up on discounted cash flow and market research. Little scraps of Virginia Woolf, D.H. Lawrence and Aldous Huxley, torn bleeding from novels rich in grammar and vocabulary, are flung at bright seventeen-year-olds. They bring them to me with a bottle of the local product, for a hand with their homework. A nice easy pastime that. It takes me back to the good old days when languages were taught in studious boredom with chalk, blackboards, exercise books, and explanations in the pupils' mother tongue. No one was expected to chatter in a barbarous lingo except vulgar couriers and seedy commercial travellers. In those peaceful days there were no language labs, no tapes, no bits of wire, no Stakhanovite teachers yearning to impart the gift of the gab to pupils who would be so much nicer if mute and modest. Silence, blotting paper and the scratch of old-fashioned pen-nibs!

'Oh no!' says Sophie, waving a pretty foot in new luxuriously simple sandals. 'Think of the money!'

Like Mussolini, Sophie is always right.

Le Monde, 3rd July 1983

[Now there are two daarlin' words. Prosopagnosia is absent from the Shorter Oxford Dictionary, but it gives prosopalgia; facial neuralgia; face-ache. If you become almost anything in France – a pupil at school, an MP, a car driver, a foreign resident – you have to hand over a number of photographs of your *trombine*, slang for face.

Often these get photocopied, thirty or more to the page, to form a trombinoscope (inadequately translated in the big Harrap dictionary as a 'rogues' gallery'). All good French offices that deal with people en masse have trombinoscopes. Teachers, for example, find them handy when they have to write reports or meet parents and would like to know who the hell they are supposed to be passing judgement upon. When prosopagnosia joins the inability to recall names it is time to retire.]

Holy James Shell

(*As printed in* Le Monde. *Homage and apologies to Miles Kington*)

Agde, la terrasse d'une mini-brasserie.

CLIENT: Garçong!

GARÇON: Yes sir! Angliche spoking!

CLIENT: Oh jolly good. Are there any baked beans on toast?

GARÇON: Euh . . . angliche menu here. Regard.

CLIENT: Très bon, très bon. Cher Dieu, qu'est que c'est que Holy James Shell?

GARÇON: Holy James Shell, very good. 40 francs. She is a cadeau.

CLIENT: Oui, mais quoi?

GARÇON: Shell, shell. Comme the essence – the pétrole.

CLIENT: Montrez. Ciel, c'est un scallop.

GARÇON: Scallop? But I have dictionary in pocket. I traduit all the menu avec. Caramba, quel arbeit. See: coquille, shell; saint, holy; Jacques, James. You are véritable Angliche? I pay dictionary 25 francs, he is one good dictionary.

CLIENT: C'est un scallop. Très dangereux sur le continent.

GARÇON: But they are angliches scallops! Congelés, from Ecosse!

CLIENT: Où?

GARÇON: Ecosse. Is in Angleterre.

CLIENT: Jamais entendu. Exeter? Eccles?

GARÇON: No, Ecosse. I search in dictionary. Voilà: Scotland! Is in Angleterre, no?

CLIENT: No. Absolument no. Et si vous pensez que j'ai venu tout le distance de Kensington à Agde pour manger un frozen scallop de Scotland, vous avez un autre pensée à venir, mon ami.

GARÇON: I suggère zigs of frogs at the provençal.

CLIENT: Zigs of frogs? Où est the English menu? Aoh, thighs of frogs. It is pronounced thighs. Repeat: thighs.

GARÇON: Saïsse.

CLIENT: Pas mauvais. Encore.

GARÇON: Saïze.

CLIENT: OK pour maintenant. Mais nous ne disons pas thighs of frogs. C'est frogs' legs, grenouilles' jambes. A London c'est pour les yuppies, pour impressionner leurs popsies. Une popsie, c'est une petite dame très expen-

sive. Les restaurants anglais ne disent pas frogs' legs mais cuisses de grenouilles, c'est plus distinguished en français. Les lower-middles ont des lobsters congelés made in Singapore. Les frogs' legs, c'est importé de France.

GARÇON: Ici, c'est from Hong Kong.

CLIENT: Pas de legs congelés pour moi, même arqués, ho ho ho. Avez-vous sausage et – où est votre dictionary? – euh . . . et écrasé?

GARÇON: What is sausage?

CLIENT: Quelle une question! Regardez à travers la rue, ce shop, CHARCUTERIE. C'est plein de sausages. Sausages noirs, sausages blancs, sausages roses.

GARÇON: Ah si! Ja! I have sausage. But écrasé? What is?

CLIENT: Mashed. Sausage and mashed, bon Dieu. Potatoes. Vous bouillez, puis vous écrasez. Voilà, c'est dans le dictionary. To mash, écraser.

GARÇON: M'at last, I have ras the bowl of this dictionary. Patates écrasées, c'est de la purée. Good, we have in sachet. Fast food, hein?

CLIENT: OK alors. Sausage et écrasé. Et un pot de tea.

GARÇON: Un pot de quoi? We have réserve du patron, château aramon de la plaine, very good, very natural . . .

CLIENT: No, tea.

GARÇON: You espel? Say letters?

CLIENT: Ti, i, é.

GARÇON: Hélas . . . You escrive? Take my Bic.

CLIENT: OK regardez: T E A.

GARÇON: Té! Euh! Ah! Au sacred dictionary . . .

Le Monde, 24th October 1982

[*M'at last* = *m'enfin*, familiar for *mais enfin*, a vague noise equivalent to 'oh well'. *J'ai ras le bol* = my bowl is brimful = 'I'm fed up'. 'At the', for *à la* (cookery), occurs when the translator's study of English has not got much further than the purchase of a pocket dictionary. I have found 'Nets of herring at the oil' (*filets de hareng à l'huile; filet* = net or fillet). 'Holy James Shell' and 'Thighs of frogs at the provençal' are genuine. I have seen 'Grown Ham' in Avignon, for raw ham (of the expensive Parma sort); good A-levellists will appreciate that the translator is not brilliant at his own language (*crû*, past participle of *croître*, to grow, and *cru*, raw). Let's be fair: the situation is no better, vice versa, in 'French' restaurants in the UK when the waiters are Portuguese, the cook comes from Nicosia and the boss from Cricklewood.]

TRYING TO INSTRUCT THE BRITISH

The articles that follow, like the ones from *Le Monde*, are chosen from my 'village' output. But I wrote them in English – an easier job, in one way, but harder in another. If one lives abroad one gets out of touch with the day-to-day preoccupations of English readers. Take monkfish, for example: it never dared show its ugly mug in a British fishmonger's before Sophie and I emigrated in 1975. In 1980, I wrote a book for Britons who rent self-catering accommodation in France, praising the creature's rear end – only to find on a flying visit that monkfish-and-chips (not to mention squid-and-chips) had become as British as taramasalata. Similarly, a few years ago, I was asking 'What is a Gazza?' (a football player, as if you didn't know). A more eminent exile, Anthony Burgess, suffered the same symptoms on reading that something or other had 'gotta lotta bottle.' This leads to a loss of fluent confidence, except of course in Mr Burgess's case.

February

MIMOSA is blooming in golden-yellow swags in sheltered gardens, and around the vineyards the almond trees are in full flower.

All the same, February is the coldest month of the year down here, fifteen miles from the Med. Our back garden is really a walled courtyard, but the north wind sweeps into it directly from the frozen Massif Central mountains two or three days a week, causing whichever one of us is hanging out the clothes to rush back muttering about brass monkeys. Local estate agents tend to boast about our micro-climate; no *mistral* (that's the north wind which blows down the Rhône valley at 80 mph to the east of us) and no *tramontane* (near the Pyrenees, on our west, more like 90 mph). True enough, but they don't mention *our* wind, the *terral*. It's only about 70 mph though . . .

But we do have our *cagnard*, the little private basking place, out of the wind and in the sun, at the top of the flight of steps leading to our front door. But there isn't room for two. (Slight squabble over the typewriter here: guess which one of us is hanging out the clothes? Guess which one of us is sipping her/his aperitif in the *cagnard* while the other is cooking the lunch? No, no, we do share life's chores fairly equally; on the other hand there are things – like basking? – which one of us does better than the other.)

On October evenings you need a fire, and in February you need all-day heat. Spells of heating will be essential right up until early May, because there's no spring in the English sense down here – winter (sunny but cold) flips into summer (sunny and hot) and back again from March onwards. Fifteen years or so ago most of the locals installed oil-fired heating, and began regretting it soon after when the petrol crisis arrived and prices soared. But older houses here have big kitchens, where life tends to be lived when it's parky in other rooms, and most people were sensible enough not to listen when enthusiastic modernisers told them to do away with the traditional wood-burning open fireplace (about six feet long). You can keep a fire going day and night in one of these: it warms your living-space and does some of the cooking. Iron pots in the embers for stews; baked potatoes in their skins (wrapped in foil nowadays) under the ash; frying pans on a trivet over the flames. Steaks and chops grill beautifully, with a little care.

So, if you have wood-gathering time to spare and a good ground-floor 'cellar' to store the wood in, you can heat yourself almost free. Vine-wood is splendid fuel. Grapes grow on the wood of the year, so from after the grape harvest until March the job is to prune away all the old branches, leaving seven or eight 'eyes' on the stump to make branches for the next crop. There are more trimmed-off branches than anyone could ever burn; four or five feet long, they make neat, easy-to-carry bundles, and any grape-grower will let you have for free as many as you care to take. These are good for a quick blaze, and ideal for summer outdoor barbecues.

But for a good solid all-night glow, you need vine-

stumps. A vine will go on producing grapes for twenty or thirty years. The three-foot-high stump from which the year's branches grow goes on getting thicker and knobblier and twistier. At last the whole vineyard gets grubbed out (a big job, this: the roots run tremendously deep, which is why vines can flourish without summer rain). The wood is hard, and burns almost like coal. If you ask nicely you can usually get a trailer-load or two dumped outside the cellar door. Free again, but this time it's usual to give a little present in return (a bottle of whisky from us; we hardly ever drink it, finding the local wine suits us better, but the natives think whisky very chic for special occasions – so whenever we've been to England we keep our 'duty-free' for such purposes). Awkward shapes, vine-stumps; they can't be cut up into neat logs, so that's why you need a big fireplace and lots of storage-room.

February is the cruellest month. Groans, pocket calculators and Form 2042 – the blue income tax form. Social security contributions get deducted at source, but for income tax they send you a bill, and oh, how it hurts! We've stopped telling the French that their income tax is a flea bite compared with the pound of flesh that the Inland Revenue hacks off the British tax payer, because it doesn't seem to make them feel any better. The dreaded blue form is no slouch, as forms go, with all those little loopholes and allowances for this and that, unknown to the stern British tax man. It has to be sent off by the end of the third week of February, and wrestling with it fills many a long winter evening.

A friend of ours who teaches history at the nearby market town was delighted to hear that the British tax year starts on the 6th April, because he likes to think that foreigners are odd, especially the English. A week later he had a theory: in 1752 we British stopped having New Year's Day towards the end of March, and dropped 11 days from that year to bring ourselves into line with the Continent; he suggests that the Treasury has not yet got around to this new-fangled calendar, and he may be right.

Talking of keeping the house warm – what you spend on insulation can come off your (French) taxable income. Which one of us has mislaid those receipts for glass fibre?

August

SOPHIE narrowly escaped being flattened the other day by 17 stones of human flesh. She was in town at the supermarket (special offer of imported Oxford marmalade). In the check-out queue there was this outsize young Dutchman, naked except for bathing shorts almost hidden under a belly sprouting curly ginger hair, who suddenly crashed to the floor. Sophie and her neighbours (locals, therefore properly dressed) managed to skip aside in time. Nobody was trapped under the steaming orange mound.

It was a touch of heatstroke, of course. He lay there for a minute, amid cries of the French equivalent of 'Ooh, it did give me a turn'; then, a little paler, he hoisted himself up, accepted a glass of water (compliments of a worried management) and toddled away, all smiles, to the campsite.

Back at the village, Sophie found John in the square,

chatting with Pélagie Bezombes on the bench in the shade of the mulberry tree. Shade or not, we all had our hats on, of course – you can't be too careful.

'Why?' asked Pélagie (a stout party herself, in her late fifties, who has a terrace overlooking most of the village and keeps a keen eye and ear on all the goings-on). 'Why are northerners so queer?' That was nice of her, proving we don't really count as foreigners any more, whereas Parisians certainly do. 'Look there!' she said, pointing to the holiday villa that the Wilkinsons from Slough have taken for a fortnight. 'They've got their windows open, and their shutters too, at midday, in this heat.' It was 95°F in the shade . . .

When it's warmish – say 90° in the shade – you keep the windows open but close the shutters. When it's hotter you shut the windows too. People like to come indoors and say, 'Aah! Nice and cool!', so they keep the hot air out, and open up in the evening. The air in the Wilkinson's place, when they return from the beach, will be as hot as the air outside and the tiled floor will have been heated by the sun. Not that the Wilkinson's will mind, perhaps. They *wanted* it hot.

What puzzles Pélagie is the Wilkinsons' time-table: no siesta. In the summer, people here get up at dawn (or earlier) and hope to be back home by 11, after five or six hours' work in the open. We finish our gardening by nine. Pélagie has done her sheets and smalls at the open-air *lavoir*, and hung them on the municipal washing lines long before seven in the delicious cool of the morning – and brought them in, dry, before ten. In the evening, life starts again. It's holiday time now, so the village children will be playing in the square till near midnight. After a bit more outdoor work, the village adults will also still be up – playing *pétanque*, going to firework displays (the 14th July was the big day for these, but they go on here and there until the end of August), village fairs and open-air dances.

So when do we catch up on sleep? We have a siesta after a good midday meal (at 12 here; after 11 you don't say *bonjour* but *bon appétit*) and we have it behind the shutters in a nice cool house. During that quiet lazy time the Wilkinsons, who missed the beauty of the sunrise and whose children will be sent to bed while it's still light, are playing beach cricket in the glare on a Mediterranean shore.

Well, it's a free country. And the Wilkinsons are nice people and say they're having the best holiday they've ever had.

We're glad, by the way, that when the Wilkinsons go into town to do their shopping they don't do it in bathing costumes. It may be all right to stroll down Oxford Street in a bikini in a heatwave, but in these backward parts, navels and suchlike, away from beach, river and lake, are exposed only by prawn-red grockles who don't mind advertising themselves as such.

Grockles? That's Cornish for tourists, or was when we were there. Pélagie is fond of grockle-watching. There are seven holiday villas (*gîtes ruraux*) in our village, so that in the summer there are about twenty-five grockles added to the normal population. We are ex-grockles now, and do our watching with the villagers in the shade. If given a chance (all a grockle has to do is say *bonjour* and smile) the villagers fraternize and give advice, tomatoes, melons, wine and grapes.

Northern French grockles begin in July and disappear all at once at the end of August, causing splendid traffic jams on the Motorway of the Sun. Scandinavian, German, Dutch and British grockles appear in April, and childless British ones can be seen up to the end of October. The ones who come to the village mostly take an interest in the local way of life. It's different down by the coast, where there are enormous highly-organized camp sites, and booths selling candy floss and chips to the British, sauerkraut and sausage to the Germans. There's a fair amount of *le topless* (and more) on those beaches too. Grockle-watching for all tastes . . .

October

THE New Year will begin about the middle of this month. The grape year, that is, when the last bunch has gone to the winery, and people start thinking about what to do to ensure a good vintage next year.

It's been like that since long before Julius Caesar, when the Romans used to import great boatloads of good honest plonk from our village and round about. That horrid emperor Diocletian tried to impose a quota on the stuff to protect Italian wine-growers – Common Market squabbles are an old story.

We always give a hand in our neighbour Henri Poujol's vineyard for a week, just to feel we belong. The first time we did it, we thought: how romantic! There we were, at seven in the morning, with a splendid view of the mountains on one side, and the Mediterranean across the plain on the other . . . And we bent down and snipped off a big juicy purple-black bunch, and dropped it into a plastic bucket; and straightened up and admired the view again . . . and noticed that Henri and his wife and his Mum and Dad and the three Spaniards who had come from Estremadura for the vintage had all *filled* their buckets, and another Spanish worker was emptying them into a *comporte* – a wooden tub (sometimes they're plastic) which holds 80 kilos and can be wheeled along to the lorry if a strong man slips a sort of skeleton wheelbarrow under the metal lugs that stick out from the sides of the *comporte* . . . so we got on with it. Those Spaniards are horny-handed demon field workers who really need the money. And it's a year's income for Henri and his family. Bend down, grab a bunch, chop it off quick, chuck it in the bucket, and repeat. And repeat. Etc. That's one stump done, in under a minute. Bucket nearly full? Yell 'Bucket' and the bucket-carrier will give you an empty one and trot off to the *comporte* with the full one. Don't stop, don't look round. Keep bending, keep cutting, keep calling 'Bucket'. Soon there are 13 *comportes* full, about a ton, and Henri drives them off in the lorry to the winery, while we keep on cutting.

It's getting hot. Sticky juice picks up dust, grit, earth. Sticky hands, face, other parts. Don't mind the wasps. Bucket! Ow, my back! When is the tea-break?

But there is no tea-break. Are these people human? There they are, the swine, bent double, zooming along the rows, and cheerful with it . . . Are they pulling your leg? I mean, one can do without tea, as such, but what about a glass of lemonade? Don't they have ice-cream vans in this country? What about a cigarette in the shade of that fig-tree, just to get the spine unbent? *Bucket!* Sweaty, sticky, itchy, thirsty.

Well, it's quite all right to eat a bunch of grapes if you don't slow down. It isn't thirst you'll die of. Effort, St Swithin's! Play up and play the game! Think of Mrs Thatcher! And the British Grenadiers! That little Spanish girl, she can't be more than thirteen, is twenty vine-stumps ahead . . . Catch up!

By mid-October the Midi's Spaniards have gone home by special train, counting their earnings. The British have gone too – students, these, and a few unemployed. Some of them pack it in after a couple of days. They have romantic notions of leisurely grape-snipping to the sound of the old guitar, and of Latin snogging in the moonlight. The survivors aren't the toughest-looking. Big rugby forwards have tottered off with stories about phone calls from dying aunts, while frail typists and retired dentists have kept the flag flying, turned nut-brown in the process, made friends and sworn to come back next year.

She, February, August and October 1984

And Now we have Naming of Streets

THE edict has come from Paris or somewhere: our streets must have names. The municipal council (nine members, thus eleven per cent of the population) spent most of their last meeting surrounded by samples of name-plates. They adjourned at a deadlock: austere economy, elegant sobriety and multi-coloured gaiety had three champions each. Later they will have to choose the names. That should occupy them for many another long winter evening.

There seems no need to hurry. From the middle ages until the 1930s the population of this village numbered about two hundred. They got on well enough without street names. Now we are down to eighty, but you can't stop progress. We have neon street lighting, main drainage and a GIVE WAY sign where the avenue of plane trees joins a very minor road, so street names had to come.

It's easy to see what will happen.

'Euh, pardon, Madame. I'm looking for *la rue Alphonse Machin-Truc . . .*'

'Well, you've come to the wrong village, young man. This is Saint-Fulcran-de-Fobis. You must want Saint-Fulcran-de-Pouzolles. It's on the other side of the hill, five kilometres away. Go down that road . . .'

That has long been a familiar dialogue here. The other

Saint-Fulcran is a great big *agglomération* of three hundred inhabitants and has had street names for ages. Great big names too: pioneer airmen and men of letters – not that the inhabitants go in for flying or for reading many books per week. You go down the *Boulevard Saint-Exupéry*, six houses long and just wide enough for a furniture van to scratch its ribs luxuriously, and then you can choose among the *Impasse Jean Racine*, the *Avenue Louis Blériot* and the *Boulevard Marcel Proust*, the far end of which is a madeleine's throw from the *Place Jean Mermoz*. (A really well-thrown madeleine would sail across the *Allée Honoré de Balzac*, go down the *Avenue Gustave Flaubert* and land well inside the postman's vineyard.)

Of course nobody uses those names. The only people who are aware of them are observant visitors. The inhabitants go on living, as they have always done, opposite the post office or next door to the grocer's. We, on the other hand, in our own Saint-Fulcran, are only too used to the puzzled enquiries of salesmen and debt-collectors who have stopped at the wrong village.

'No, no, Madame, the address really is Saint-Fulcran-de-Fobis. I'm looking for Monsieur Jean Planchais, *rue* . . .'

'Oh well, why didn't you say so? You go down the road to the cemetery, turn right by the rubbish container, and it's the first house on the left, the one with the fossilized giant oysters round the door. You can't miss it.'

So *la petite Place* will remain *la petite Place*, when we need to distinguish it from *la grande Place* (as for example when the mobile butcher has stopped his van there because *la grande Place* is totally occupied by three parked cars). But what will curious strangers see on the name plates: *Place de l'Eglise* or *Place de la Mairie*? Or, to remain neutral in the still-smouldering lay/clerical battle, *Place de la Cabine Téléphonique*?

I'm a bit of a snob about this. When Nancy Mitford was writing about U and non-U I learnt that the best addresses have the form:

J. Smith Esq
Thing House
Thing

But personally I prefer the total U-ness of:

The Archbishop
Canterbury

or

The Akond
Swat

And since I've lived in this village, I've enjoyed similar stark arrogance. Soon I shall have to join the rank and file and live in Something Street. Number One? Perhaps a mere Number 2, as there are two houses in my street. I can't hope for the *Promenade des Anglais*, either, because Madame Vidal and her daughter have lived next door for eighty-five and sixty-seven years respectively, and you might say it's their street.

Of course I shan't tell my friends the name, whatever it turns out to be.

The Times, 5th January 1984

[Six months after this was written the name-plates went up. *La grande Place* became *la Place de la Mairie*. In case that annoyed the Church party, a street off the *Place* – my street – was called after Saint Baudile. I haven't been able to find out much about this saint, but he's well known here because the relay that the village gets its television from is on top of a small mountain named after him. When there's a thunderstorm over that way the screen goes blank, and tiny tots are dismayed to find that Saint Baudile is sensitive to weather.]

Huntin' and Shootin'

A FAIR amount of chuntering is heard in France these days about law 'n' order. Not that the crime rate has shot up, but the opposition tends to blame the government for almost everything, from murder to dull TV shows, and the extreme right – recently noticeable because of the able oratory of its Duce, Monsieur Le Pen – has a *bête noire* in the person of the Minister of Justice, Robert Badinter, whom it regards as a wet because he abolished the guillotine.

However, the government proclaims that it really would like people to obey the law, so one may assume that everybody welcomed the comeuppance recently meted out to a wicked young man at the *tribunal de grande instance* of Albi. He had been awaiting trial since early June, when he was caught slinking from a wood concealing several dozen succulent snails.

The close season for snails, as every British sportsman going to France should know, runs from 1st April to 30th June. In that time snails are supposed to get on with courtship, mating, gestation, egg-laying and hatching (or snailbirth and suckling, as the case may be – I am not very well up on gastropods) without being distracted by anxieties about kidnappers.

Then on the Glorious First of July, the wild snail season opens. The chase is on, all true huntsmen hope for a fine drizzle that will tempt the game to break cover, and the woods and hills are alive with the squelch or squish of specimens being separated from the surfaces to which they had been adhering.

You can get snails all the year round in French restaurants, but nowadays they are imported from Eastern Europe, generally ready cooked in tins. The eager tourist at a five-star French hotel de luxe who orders a couple of lightly-boiled fresh local snails for breakfast during the close season gets the same dusty answer as he would at the Savoy Grill if he asked for grouse before 12th August.

Few Frenchmen know, by the way, that there is no close season for *la chasse aux escargots* in England's green and, in normal years, pleasantly damp land. Wake up, British Tourist Authority!

The Albi court fined the snail poacher 500 francs (about £45), and awarded one franc symbolic damages (all it asked for) to the Fédération Départementale de Chasse. But even at Albi, where heretics got a short sharp deal in the twelfth century, signs of wetness have seeped in: the sentence was suspended. I hope the young man will have the good sense to spend next spring on a law-abiding safari around Chipping Sodbury, where there is good snailing.

A propos de hunting etc, let me bring to the surface a cutting from *Le Monde* of October last year, on the delights of shooting and fishing in Ireland.

The keen Frenchman (having written two letters to Dublin at least a month in advance, one with 10 Irish pounds enclosed, to the Department of Justice asking for permission to import his fowling-piece, the other to the Forest and Wild Life Service requesting a shooting licence) can have enormous fun from November to

March when, the article alleges, *canaris, sarcelles et bécasses* abound.

Yes, that's right: canaries, teal and woodcock.

I wrote to *Le Monde* to express my regret that such an eminent paper, normally a wholesome influence, should encourage its readers to join in the regrettable Irish habit of bagging these charming little songsters. It may be all right for natives in their turf cabins to eke out the boiled potatoes with a brochette or two of such *uccellini* and a noggin of poteen before getting back to the Celtic dream-twilight on pillows stuffed with tiny yellow feathers. They have been brought up to it. But would not even Tartarin de Tarascon have drawn the line at a *canari?*

It turned out to be one of *Le Monde's* very rare misprints. For *canaris* read *canards*. But I assure you that the Albi trial really was about real snails.

The Times, 15th November 1984

[1992: Monsieur Le Pen, looking more and more like a cross between Mussolini and Benny Hill, continues to orate. Monsieur Badinter is no longer Minister of Justice, but pursues a distinguished career elsewhere. Capital punishment has not been restored. Ready-stuffed snails are available all the year round from the deep freeze. *Canards* are ducks.]

The six-sided language

[WE British are less easily worked up about the past, present and future of what a headmaster I suffered under always called 'the old parlay-voo' than are French editors and their readers, but there is a market for articles on the subject. I have taken three of my pieces that *The Times* published (in 1983 and 1984) and shaken them up.]

It must be a century since subeditors, seeing the word oysters three times in a paragraph, felt obliged to cross it out twice, substituting 'delicious bivalves' and 'succulent molluscs'. The reverse happens today. Woolly bleaters, finny denizens of the deep and web-footed waddlers are out, and nobody minds seeing a word twice in a dozen lines. But elegant variation is still a conditioned reflex among French journalists from *Le Monde* to *Midi-Libre*.

Let's consider reports that fluctuations of the green note are causing trouble in the bosom of the hexagon.

The green note, *le billet vert*, is the dollar. It will almost certainly remain the green note if the US Treasury issues dollars in luminescent orange or as aluminium discs. The sequence, perhaps now programmed into French word-processors, is 1) *le dollar*, 2) *le billet vert*, 3) *la devise américaine*, the American currency; then 4) *le dollar*, and off we go again.

The hexagon is France. Well, yes, the map can be seen as showing six shakily-drawn sides. This is convenient, because a hexagon is thought to be the right shape for a country. Norway is too frayed at the edges, Spain is too square, and Great Britain is no shape at all. (Besides, it is wholly surrounded by salty, choppy water – almost as bad as the equally shapeless and landlocked Switzerland. France has neither of those drawbacks. It has also cleverly avoided being too big, like the United States, or too small, like Holland.) The hexagon is just right, or would be if only there were mountains along that historically awkward Belgian border.

The bosom, *le sein*, can cause problems to the non-hexagonal reader. *Un sein* is a breast, normally occurring as one of a pair. If you hide something in your *sein* you tuck it in your brassière. When the French are trying to purge themselves of *le franglais* they talk of *seins nus* instead of *le topless*. As every French schoolboy once knew, Etienne Carjat said in 1879 that the Revolution was the male wet-nurse that suckled Gambetta (the founder of the Third Republic) at his, or her, or its virile *sein*.

But it can also be a womb, where the foetus or bright idea or revolution is gestating. Hexagonal ladies can thus boast three *seins*, and if something is said to be in someone's or something's *sein* it can be inside, or vaguely around somewhere.

So *au sein de l'hexagone* just means *en France*. But the chap couldn't say *en France* because he had said it already, twelve lines above.

Other possessors of one or more *seins* liable to agitation are OTAN and the CEE (NATO and the EEC, hexagonalized like *le talkie-walkie* – though oddly enough *le ping-*

pong remains as in *la langue de Shakespeare,* which believe it or not is what this article is written in), the French international rugby team, 10 Downing Street and of course Buckingham (which is French for Buckingham Palace).

Let us be quite clear. No one is supposed to register the bald meaning of substitute-words. They function as mere pronouns. No eyebrow is raised when letters are reported to have come in 'from the four corners of the hexagon'. The other day my local paper said that the area round Lake Salagou had become 'an hexagonal Arizona for film-makers'. That means it is useful for rugged location shots.

Originality is taboo. The reader does not have to think. *Le métal précieux* and *le métal jaune* are compulsory for *l'or,* gold. Dragging in ductility, malleability or solubility in aqua regia would not be playing the game. The porcine, bovine and ovine races are pigs, cattle and sheep. Inflorescences, tubers and palmipeds stand in for cauliflowers, potatoes and ducks. When a bear escaped near my home in the Midi, the local paper swung effortlessly into action with *l'ours, l'animal* and *le plantigrade.*

Well-known politicians have similar conventional aliases, and beginners in the study of the French press long for an ad hoc dictionary. If you read that Monsieur Machin insulted Monsieur Untel, the Mayor of Gateau-Saint-Honoré slapped the Mayor of Coquilles-Saint-Jacques, and the MP for Demain-en-Principe kicked the shins of the MP for Foie-de-Veau, there are probably only two people involved. I am sure that Michel Rocard, a man with a future, has some distinguished aliases to come; years ago it took me a long while to realize that not only *le député des Yvelines* but also *le maire de Conflans-Saint-Honorine* (who kept on turning up) were none other than he.

The semicircle, *l'hémicycle*, is parliament (aka *le palais Bourbon*). The French chamber has the shape denounced by Churchill when the rebuilding of our own blitzed House was under discussion: 'The semi-circular assembly . . . enables every individual or group to move around the centre, adopting various shades of pink as the weather changes.' If you have followed me so far, you will see why it was natural for *Le Monde*'s London correspondent, one day in the eighties, to report that *la Dame de Fer* (Mrs Thatcher) had been addressing *l'hémicycle britannique*. The man knew it was oblong, but he had used *la chambre* two lines above. Or perhaps it was a subeditor on auto-pilot.

Journalistic jargon of that sort does not worry the Establishment. Eminent bodies such as the Académie Française, the Comité Consultatif de la Langue Française and the Commissariat Général de la Langue Française devote their efforts to counter-offensives against Anglo-Saxon cultural and linguistic imperialism. Quasi-Italian noises may be heard in the *Ile de Beauté* (otherwise Corsica) and a lot of Arabic in *la cité phocéenne* (Marseilles, founded by the Phocaeans; all French newspaper readers and telly watchers know this alias, while hardly one in a hundred has heard of the Phocaeans), but the sacred groves of the Académie Française are in a state of active defence against the descendants of Hengist and Horsa.

Representative Anglo-Saxons, in the eyes of the Establishment, are Frank Sinatra, Rabbie Burns, Louis Armstrong and anyone whose name begins with O'. Articles on The Anglo-Saxon Cinema are about Roman Polanski or *Gone with the Wind* (it keeps coming back) rather than some primitive silent epic on the Beowulf theme. Anglo-Saxon linguistic infiltration and sabotage are fiercely combated by *l'Establishment*. Edicts, hastily formulated in the *seins* of ministries of this and that, try to stop business schools talking about *le marketing, le cash-flow* and *le joint-venture*. TV people must stop calling a voice off *une voix off*. I do my best to obey. I went to the shop to buy a correcting ribbon for my typewriter yesterday, and asked for *un ruban de correction par soulèvement*. 'Ah,' said the wicked assistant, '*Vous voulez un lift-off*.'

There is a vast palace of rock music in a Paris suburb, opened in 1984 by none other than President Mitterrand. It was to be called Le Crystal, but while they were putting the finishing touches to it, a high authority (*Le Monde* thought it was Monsieur Mitterrand himself) found in that name *une tonalité anglo-saxonne*. They have delicate nuance-sniffers over here. *Cristal* is a good old French word; the *y* must have been the Anglo-Saxon in the woodpile. The hall was obediently dubbed Le Zénith. The word is of Arabic origin, and is also the name of an inexpensive Russian camera, but perhaps the patriotic acute accent tipped the scales.

All this cuts no ice with your younger member of the lower class. *Le rapp* resounds from his *hi-fi* while he chews his *hamburger*. He is clad in *un tee-shirt* and a pair of *jean's*. Yes, *jean's* with an apostrophe, like *le pin's*, which means an enamelled badge. Decorative apostrophes are very much *in* (pronounced 'een').

The Establishment has a cavalier attitude to other languages. When you see *des spaghettis* on the menu, don't sneer at the staff. The Académie Française has ruled that this is the correct plural, hexagonally speaking. The same goes for *confettis, lasagnes* and *graffitis*. I tell you no lie: the singular is *un graffiti*. They wince when a foreigner says *générals* instead of *généraux*, or on the other hand *navaux* instead of *navals*, but the French for the media is very officially *les médias*; like *les erratas* and *les duplicatas*. So much for Latin and Italian. A rugby player is *un rugbyman*. No nonsense about that, says the Académie, and rules that the plural has to be *les rugbymans*.

But the Académie has had trouble with the Minister of Women's Rights. Every British schoolchild knows that French is a macho language. When my short-trousered little comrades and I were first told that a thousand girls plus one boy were *ils*, not *elles*, there were cries of 'Ooh sir, not fair!' Masculine for half and half, or perhaps six girls to four boys, we could accept, but one yowling male baby to a train-load of Mae Wests or (not that we had heard of her then) Mrs Thatchers, no.

We British are having problems with barpersons and ploughperson's lunches and what to call the Mayor's marital partner when the Mayor is a lady, and officialdom seems to have adopted the nasty habit of using 'they' to mean one person to avoid having to decide between 'he or she' and 'she or he'. But these are mere flea bites in comparison with the French situation. The Minister of Women's Rights had a Terminological

Commission trying to think up feminine equivalents of words like *ministre, docteur, chef, écrivain* and the like. These are all masculine in gender, while the people concerned (like *le ministre* herself) can be female in sex. No need, said the Académie: while feminine means female, masculine means the lot: *tous les hommes sont mortels,* 'all men are mortal', means the whole human race, *Les hommes* are men and women, *les femmes* are not. A female minister should be quite happy to be called *le ministre*; female doctors should not be jealous of the chemist, who can be *le pharmacien* or *la pharmacienne* according to sex.

This simply will not do. Come off it, Académie. General de Gaulle began his famous televised speeches with 'Françaises! Français!' No nonsense for him about Français doing for both sexes – he gave the Françaises their vote. And subsequent orators, left, right and centre, follow his example.

If you have led off with *le ministre* or *le docteur* you have to call that person *il,* and make all adjectives describing her (or him, as the case may be) masculine, until you can play another card disclosing the real state of things – the person's name, for example, or something like *cette femme,* after which you can get back on the rails with *elle.* The invention of words like *doctoresse, ministresse, chefesse* and *écrivaine* would help. What a difference the Channel makes! British feminists want to suppress such sex-revealing words, in the interests of the Siblinghood of Person. They do not have to cope with French grammar.

French grammar puts females at a disadvantage. Suppose you wish to write something like 'I found myself overwhelmed by letters from the four corners of the hexagon'. You scribble on your rough copy *Je me suis trouvé débordé* . . . and warning bells ring. A reflexive verb, a verb conjugated with *être* . . . Perhaps *trouvé*, or perhaps *débordé*, or perhaps both, should be made to agree with the subject. But when I say 'you', I mean you only if you are a female. The subject is *Je*. I'm all right; I can slap down *trouvé* and *debordé* without thinking, because my *Je* is masculine, and the masculine form of those words is just the same as if they didn't have to agree with anything. But you, dear lady, will have to put *trouvée* or *débordée* or both or neither according to what you remember of your schooldays. Perhaps you will decide to telephone instead. The difference can't be heard, and you don't want to circulate written evidence that could be used against you.

God bless them, all the same, *Françaises* and *Français*. They do care about their language. From semioticians to horny-handed journalists, from poets to politicians, they worry about it with untiring passion, and are amazed that Anglo-Saxons just let their lingo go marching on regardless.

The Times, 18th August 1983, 23rd February 1984 and 16th July 1984

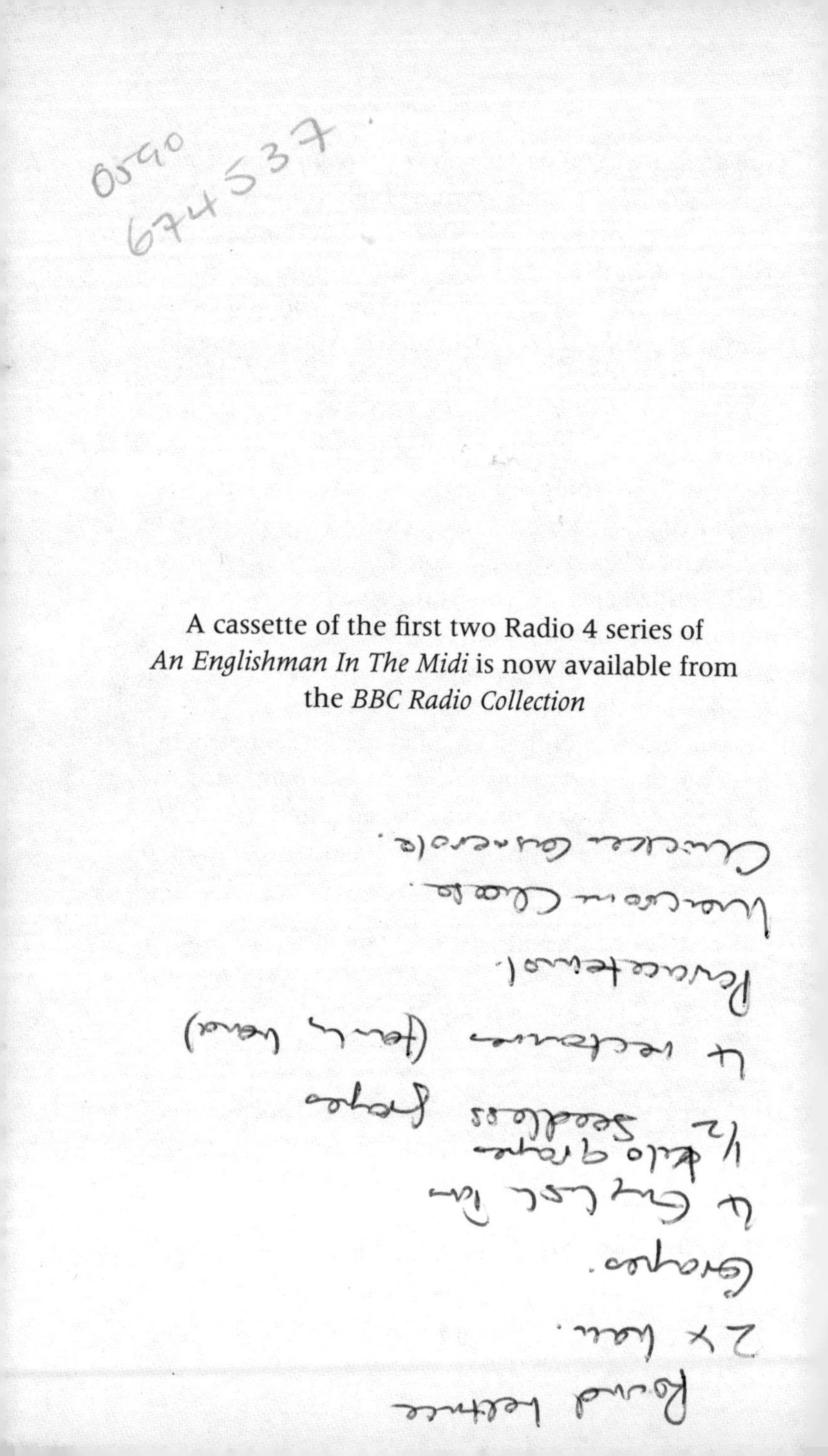

0590
674537

A cassette of the first two Radio 4 series of *An Englishman In The Midi* is now available from the *BBC Radio Collection*